T0153016

Theories of Practice

Other Redleaf Press Books by Carol Garhart Mooney

Theories of Childhood: An Introduction to Dewey, Montessori, Erikson, Piaget, and Vygotsky, second edition

Theories of Attachment: An Introduction to Bowlby, Ainsworth, Gerber, Brazelton, Kennell, and Klaus

Swinging Pendulums: Cautionary Tales for Early Childhood Education

Use Your Words: How Teacher Talk Helps Children Learn

Theories of Practice

Raising the Standards of Early Childhood Education

Carol Garhart Mooney

Redleaf Press®
www.redleafpress.org
800-423-8309

Published by Redleaf Press
10 Yorkton Court
St. Paul, MN 55117
www.redleafpress.org

First edition 2015
Cover design by Jim Handrigan
Cover illustration by Ian Handrigan, age 4
Interior design by Douglas Schmitz
Typeset in Kandal
Printed in the United States of America
21 20 19 18 17 16 15 14   1 2 3 4 5 6 7 8

Library of Congress Cataloging-in-Publication Data

Mooney, Carol Garhart.
  Theories of practice : raising the standards of early childhood
education / Carol Garhart Mooney.
       pages cm
  Summary: "With stories, anecdotes, and a discussion about the strong
connection between theory and best practices, this guide will help you
understand the value of applying your knowledge of educational theory to
your work as you refine your practices, create thoughtful curriculum, and
do your best to raise the standards of early childhood education"—Provided by
publisher.
  Includes bibliographical references and index.
  ISBN 978-1-60554-287-4 (paperback)
  ISBN 978-1-60554-297-3 (e-book)
1. Early childhood education--Philosophy. 2. Early childhood
education—Curricula. I. Title.
  LB1139.23.M65 2014
  372.21—dc23
                              2014025122
Printed on acid-free paper

To Marc, for everything

Contents

Foreword

IN THIS BOOK, ONCE AGAIN, Carol Garhart Mooney shares with us her rich insights based on extensive experience of working in the complex and challenging provisions for the care and education of young children. Throughout her analyses and discussions of the day-to-day challenges and complexities involved in early childhood education, she helps us to grasp the important contribution of how we understand the nature of our work—its responsibilities and the potential consequences of our theories (some conscious and others not necessarily so) of how our practices work.

Mooney also examines what she refers to as a "disconnect" between the important theories of development and learning, and how our daily practices often fail to apply the vast and growing amount of relevant knowledge now available. Her discussions carry a strong emphasis on the importance of the theoretical bases of our work. As she puts it: "More than ever, people working with young children and their families need education and understanding of child growth and development" (17). She strongly supports the view that an important attribute of a teacher is that she or he is also a learner . . . a constant learner—not only from firsthand experience, but also from the growing body of related information and knowledge in the field.

In addition to her very useful references to the theories and the expanding knowledge base related to early childhood education and child rearing in the early years, Mooney presents a clear and convincing position of the importance of improving early childhood education as a profession.

Mooney's main theme puts the value of theory and related hypotheses—based on reasoning—in the practical context of the daily challenges faced by practitioners in the field. Her suggestion that "no one theory is universally accepted as *the* theory of how and why children grow and learn as they do" (28) is followed by the very useful suggestion that practitioners at every level of responsibility and at various levels of qualifications are likely to gain greatly from constant interactions and reflections with their colleagues.

While the title of this work seems to emphasize theory, Mooney makes it clear that *practice* refers directly to the ways we respond (or fail to respond) to the children who are with us. She makes the point that surely all practices are based on theories and related hypotheses—but not necessarily appropriate ones. It is most likely that the majority of practitioners in the field of early education and care are unaware of the theoretical bases of many of their actions.

Every page raises and explores many of the frequent practical challenges practitioners face day-to-day. Reading Mooney's exploration of the implications of various theories of practice is enlightening as well as provocative and enriches the growing profession of early childhood education.

—Lilian G. Katz, PhD
University of Illinois

Acknowledgments

FOR SUCH A TINY BOOK, the list of those involved is lengthy. My first thanks go to my husband, Marc, for reading, editing, IT assistance, suggestions, and final preparation, and my son, Brian Mooney, for always playing devil's advocate! Kyra Ostendorf and David Heath at Redleaf Press consistently offer answers, encouragement, and humor that keep the books coming.

This book involved continual input from direct service practitioners. High on that list are Marilyn Nicholson, Yvette Robert, Marjiana Kljajic, Kathy Trellis, and Erin Mooney. In addition, a faithful group of focus group attendees kept showing up at the end of long workdays to discuss their work with children and families. Their knowledge is extensive, their experience vast, and their commitment to early childhood education an inspiration. You know who you are. I offer my heartfelt thanks.

Thank you to the professional picnic group that, for more than three decades, has supported me and any work I get accomplished. Thanks especially to Sara, Tessa, Cindy, Karen, Wendy, and Susan.

Special thanks to Cindy Wallace, Tracy Pond, Claudette Mallory, and many others at New Hampshire Child Care Resource and Referral for lending support, arranging focus groups, and gathering feedback from the field every time I write.

Behind the scenes much of the time but front and center when I need information and encouragement are the people at the Child Development Bureau: Dr. Ellen Wheatley, Kristin Booth, Sue Foley, and Jessica Locke. Thanks for all you do.

xi

In small and large ways, folks at Early Learning NH and Spark NH put information in my hands and critical phone numbers on my cell phone as well as all around ECE support. These include Laura Milliken, Jackie Cowell, Katie Brissette, Brenda LaFratta, Carol Michael, Neal Scott, and especially Mary Jane Wallner, whose experience and friendship span the decades.

Pat Meattey at Strafford County Head Start has put her mark on every book I've ever written. Her expertise and sharing regarding the 2007 mandate for Head Start teachers gave me last-minute confidence about the importance of early childhood specific education and its daily impact, or not, on America's children.

My gratitude to all of you.

—Carol Garhart
Center Barnstead, New Hampshire
2014

Introduction

TEACHERS WHO STAND OUT for their excellence are usually lifelong learners. These are the women and men who keep attending conferences, workshops, discussion groups, or webinars that address continuous professional improvement and change.

These are the educators who ask:

- How could I have done that better?

- When did I lose the group?

- How can I adapt this next time to avoid the problems that came up?

- Who might be able to help me generate some solutions to this challenge?

The answer to that last question, for me, has often been Lilian Katz. I use every one of her books, journal articles, and quotes that I can find. I attend any local lectures she presents and arrange my National Association for the Education of Young Children conference schedule around her presentations. Her work has always seemed intensely cognitive and totally practical.

I have observed at conferences over the years her habit of joining groups of practitioners in the commercial exhibits or coffee areas to discuss their views of the field. It was one such instance two years ago that provided the name and underlying premise for this book. I had the good fortune to speak briefly with Dr.

1

Katz in Orlando, Florida. I had just met with my editor to discuss this book when I ran into Dr. Katz, and we chatted about the teachers she had just been speaking to about their work. She told me the biggest things on these teachers' minds were working with parents, managing children's behaviors, and negotiating their own differences of opinion on approaches to teaching.

It's the differences in approaches to teaching that I zeroed in on. I had already read and heard Dr. Katz's words about intentional teaching and the importance of meaningful interactions in classrooms. Decades ago she said that she had no problem when teachers responded to her question "What's going on here?" with an honest "Probably nothing much!" We all have days (picture day, parent meeting days, field trip days) when we know there aren't enough hours or the children lack the ability to focus on certain curriculum. So clever and intuitive teachers usually just give up and leave things loose for the rest of the day. Dr. Katz has said she finds this sensible and understandable.

Her concern begins when nothing meaningful is going on and teachers seem unaware of this fact, or worse, when nothing intellectually stimulating or engaging is available on a regular basis yet this is fine with the teachers. This reminds me of a number of supervising teachers I met when visiting students for observations in classrooms that seemed chaotic to me. The supervising teachers would enthusiastically proclaim that their schools were devoted to developmentally appropriate practice (DAP) and they never told the children what to do! This was always a frightening experience for me.

There has been much misunderstanding and misinterpretation of the sound concept of DAP. Frequently directors know what DAP is but have several classrooms in which teachers with minimal training requirements are spending their days with children. This is one of our major theory/practice breaking points. Theory is formed from certain fundamental knowledge that early childhood education (ECE) is based on. The practice of this theory can hardly occur when a (research-documented) majority of our field is unfamiliar with this knowledge base. When directors know the theory but the classroom teachers they supervise do not, the basic premise of theory-driven practice is broken.

For decades I have been interested in the value of strong theoretical foundations in producing meaningful daily practices with children. Unfortunately, my years of observation tell me that too often teachers' practices become routine or mundane and lack the foundation that makes a curriculum rich and exciting for learners.

So we hold conferences focused on merging theory and practice. We write texts about theory and practice. This book was about to be one more of them until Lilian Katz's insightful comment rearranged my thinking.

While talking with Dr. Katz that day at the conference, I told her that my next book would be called *Theories of Teaching*. It would be the third of my collection of books on theorists; the two already published ones were *Theories of Childhood* and *Theories of Attachment*. The plan for *Theories of Teaching* was to include some theorists whose work is critical to ECE but often (with a few exceptions) is not given adequate coverage in introductory texts. I told her I wanted teachers to really study the pieces—for example, temperament, multiple and emotional intelligences, and culture—that so dramatically affect our work with children and families. I think neglecting these is one reason we struggle in our attempts to connect theory and practice.

I also described a small manual (my original plan for this book) that would serve as an introduction to the three books on theorists. It would outline the reasons why learning about and caring about foundational theories are so important to implementing quality practices for children. In other words, I believed that the theory and the practice were both important.

3

Dr. Katz's initial response to all this was just one word: "Interesting!" She was quiet for a few moments, then shared her perspective that she thinks one of the problems our field faces is that we always separate theory and practice in our thinking, our talking, and our doing. "Rather than always saying 'theory *and* practice,' keeping them separate, we should probably be saying 'theories *of* practice,' merging them as in reality they are or, ideally, should be."

I was amazed at the time and continue to be by how different our models of teaching could become by changing those four letters (*-y and*) to her five letters (*-ies of*) in describing what we are trying to do. I believe theories *of* practice is an idea we need to start thinking and talking about. There are those who will argue that this is simply a matter of semantics. I think probably not. I also think, increasingly, that there is not that much about our work that can be described with the word *simply*. Because of that, there will be times when in order to address that complexity, I use *and/of* when discussing how we weave our theories in with their practices.

I use the term "our theories" because the field of ECE has been shaped by the research of many theorists and educators as well as shared ideas in related fields and disciplines. "Our theories" here refers to the body of knowledge focused on prenatal development through that of eight-year-olds, as distinct from that used in elementary education, intermediate education, or higher education.

Our theories and our practices bring to my mind the names of ECE foundational theorists whose collective works I have outlined in *Theories of Childhood*: Jean Piaget, Erik Erikson, Maria Montessori, Lev Vygotsky, and John Dewey. The body of knowledge also includes many others, such as Friedrich Froebel, Johann Pestalozzi, and Lucy Sprague Mitchell. If I speak of contemporary influences, I would surely mention Ed Zigler, David

Weikart, Jerome Kagan, T. Berry Brazelton, Lilian Katz, and Barbra Bowman, to name only a few. As ECE has increased its focus on infants and toddlers, it has encouraged review of the work of John Bowlby, Mary Ainsworth, Magda Gerber, John Kennell, and Marshall Klaus. The work of these theorists has also been previously outlined in *Theories of Attachment*. It's important to note that most of our theories are based on work in the broader disciplines of psychology and human development.

As I approached the task of writing a usable guide to merging theory and practice, to making them—when possible—one and the same, I returned again and again to the honest, thought-provoking, and sometimes plain misled discussions I have heard about teachers' day-to-day struggles with children and curriculum. I hear repeatedly from child care teachers that their days often pass without the richness of a curriculum that they truly want to provide.

This gives me optimism. It tells us that, unlike teachers who think everything is just fine when it isn't, many teachers are reflecting on their practices and finding them less than adequate. Usually acknowledging the struggle is the first step to making improvements. Most teachers who have really refined their practices, created thoughtful curriculum, and become competent at implementing it have done so over a long period of time. Their motivation is usually that they care deeply about working with young children and strive for continuous improvement.

Chapter 1: When We Don't Know Theories As Well As We Thought

IN THE WINTER OF 2013, the New Hampshire Child Care Resource and Referral (CCR&R) sponsored what was supposed to be a training series for experienced teachers on combining ECE theories with their daily practices. However, as my copresenters and I began to explore the needs and gaps in teachers' experience, the training evolved into focus groups on how teachers and programs blend theory and practice . . . or how they don't.

My copresenters and I started the first session with two very brief pretests. The first was a series of fill-in-the-blank questions (usually considered more difficult than multiple choice or matching). The first five questions were these:

1. Missing children often have photos on _____.

2. America runs on _____.

3. I saw her on _____ *with the Stars*.

4. "Drink Coke, it's the _____ thing!"

5. After eating this cake, I'll be a candidate to star on _____.

Answers: 1. milk cartons; 2. Dunkin'; 3. Dancing; 4. real; 5. The Biggest Loser

Teachers enthusiastically tallied their scores. Then they were asked to stand if they had all five correct. Then four correct, and so on. All participants had at least three out of five correct.

7

Then we gave a second pretest. It was a matching test, so all correct pairs were in plain view. The first five matches (there were ten in total) were these:

Vygotsky	Cognitive Development Theory
Erikson	Progressive Education
Gardner	Zone of Proximal Development
Piaget	Psycho-social Development
Dewey	Multiple Intelligence Theory

Again participants were asked to score their pretest, and those with all correct answers were asked to stand. No one. "All right . . . those who only missed one?" No one. "Anyone miss just two?" No one. "Wow! . . . Anyone miss three?" No one. "Anyone miss four?" Still not one participant was standing. A stunned silence fell over the group. Quite intentionally, we just let the silence hang in the air. At this point, every teacher in the room had scored at least four out of ten wrong—60 percent, or an F in most classes. Remember—these were mostly experienced teachers of young children. All of them were acknowledging a lack of appropriate understanding of our foundational theorists.

We spent the rest of the session just talking together about what had happened here and why. Responses to why the group had done so well with the first pretest included these:

- It's everywhere, in your face, on TV and radio, ads, billboards.

- People always talk about current trends and shows.

- You use the products yourself.

- Constant ads increase sales.

- Sponsors have a huge vested interest in keeping these things on our minds.

We discussed the fact that even faithful Starbucks users knew that America Runs on Dunkin' (if you live in an area without Dunkin' Donuts, you'll have to trust me that everyone in New Hampshire and other areas with Dunkin' Donuts knows this slogan). Why did the majority of respondents who correctly identified *The Biggest Loser* and *Dancing with the Stars* say they had never even watched the programs? It's been many years since Coke has been advertised as "the real thing." Why would teachers who were fifteen at the time that Coke was constantly advertising as "the real thing" remember that . . . but not major ECE foundational theorists whom they learned about only four or five years ago? The group discussed the effects of culture and advertising on the things they hold in their minds without really thinking about them.

The discussion of the second pretest was equally interesting. Participants and presenters agreed that there was a bit more angst and defensiveness during the second discussion that had been absent during the first. At one point, one of the participants said, "Sorry, I guess I really opened a can of worms!" She had put the suggestion out there that teachers do things automatically without linking them to what they learned in college. She also noted that once she opened the door to the discussion, many participants shared strong feelings. There was a fair amount of disagreement among the participants. Here are some of the responses to why the group had done so poorly on the second pretest:

- I had a terrible professor for child growth and development.

- We know what we are doing when we do it; we just don't label it.

- I was only twenty when I learned that. There were too many theorists.

- The daily connections between children, our program, and theory just aren't that clear.

- These ads, viewed in an earlier age, or even now, just end up in your brain in a mindless way, but our teaching is intentional and based on many other factors.

As an ECE instructor, I was uncomfortable with the suggestion that theorists might be as irrelevant as advertising slogans. The implication was that as students in college, the participants had memorized theorists but did not truly make connections between the work of these theorists and their own daily work with children. Most of the participants seemed to believe they had not placed theory in a meaningful context. Given their commitment to pursuing degrees in ECE, I had anticipated their serious desire to remember this information.

The implication was that as students in college, the participants had memorized theorists but did not truly make connections between the work of these theorists and their own daily work with children.

Yet many of these same teachers referenced (intentionally or not) the need for better education. One of the sadder comments was made by a devoted infant teacher who apologized for saying that most of her coteachers were just not very smart or sophisticated. (Other participants asked about the backgrounds of these teachers, and she admitted that she was the only teacher in her program who had any college training.) Though she cared deeply about improving programs for infants, she admitted that she usually did not address her colleagues' inappropriate comments or actions because she didn't want to hurt their feelings. She talked about being hopeful that modeling appropriate practices would help other staff change their own teaching behaviors. Another participant said she found her colleagues' approaches so exasperating that she was speechless.

The discussions in our focus groups that day reflect what has become a much broader problem in the ECE field: most of these teachers had several to many years of experience working with young children and their families, yet all of these teachers admitted that more often than they would wish, their desired approach and their actual implementation of ideas were too far apart. As we explored what it meant to know theory and to have good practice, we began to focus on a major concern for our field—that as ECE teachers, many of us don't know or understand the theory behind our practices.

The Root of the Problem

We cannot make our practices reflect theories that we have never learned. Memorizing foundational theories without understanding and integrating them into meaningful practices on a daily basis with young children is no different than singing the ABC song without knowing what letters are for or why they are important. Without advanced training in child growth and development, practitioners have more difficulty making experiences rich and meaningful for the children in their care. When it comes down to it, these focus group discussions were bigger than either frustration that was voiced—the "trivia" approach or the lack of college degrees. They were about the need for real learning and growing throughout our careers.

It's been fifteen years since I drafted these words for the introduction to the first edition of *Theories of Childhood*, and I find them unfortunately still true today: "It seems that we have not been successful at presenting child development as a usable tool for working with young children more effectively. Perhaps we need to take a different approach to introducing theory and its practice to the beginning student or teacher." Since then I have not stopped thinking about or talking to teachers about the discrepancies that exist between the theories of ECE and observable practices in most programs for young children—and how these are a detriment to children and our field.

The Theory/Practice Disconnect

The disconnect between our theories of what young children need (based on research, tested and expanded over time) and our actual practices is vast and extends across many of our country's programs for young children. Here are several things I have heard in the past year in the halls, classrooms, and play yards of ECE settings:

- She's just doing it to get attention (six-month-old).

- That one's a handful; lies all the time (three-year-old).

- He's a sneaky one (four-year-old).

- She's a bully (two-year-old).

- He did it on purpose (eighteen-month-old).

- She stole it from Heather's cubby (four-year-old).

- He stole it from dramatic play (four-year-old).

- She has no self-control (four-year-old).

- Don't let those two sit together—they're trouble (four-year-olds).

- She tries to control all the four-year-olds (five-year-old).

- He's got a real mean streak (two-year-old).

- She thinks if she wails all day, we'll carry her around (three-month-old).

- She's the typical "mean girl" (five-year-old).

If we were to do a person-on-the-street survey, it is my hunch that many adults in this country would not find a thing wrong with many of the above comments. I do believe that most parents of infants and toddlers would be sad and upset if they thought their infants were left to cry because caregivers thought their babies were manipulative. I feel certain their parental hope would be that someone at child care would sensitively soothe and comfort their babies. But I also have a hunch that many parents as well as providers would agree that things like lying, stealing, hitting, using materials inappropriately, to name a few behaviors, mean the same thing to four-year-olds that they do to adults.

Professionals who have studied the theories of child growth and development know that this is not the case. However, that knowledge comes from

- reading Piaget, Kohlberg, Vygotsky, Erikson, and others;

- reflecting on what we've read with professors and colleagues; and

- slowly restructuring the ways we think of and respond to children's behaviors.

13

ECE professionals who have mastered foundational theory understand how important significant adults' responses are to children in the early years (birth through age eight). They understand that children's early experiences and attachments first affect their brain growth patterns and, later, their mobility, curiosity, spirit of adventure, and inquiry. An interactive effect also greatly affects how young children view themselves and how they perceive others view them. Infants' sense of basic trust develops well when a sensitive primary caregiver consistently responds to their cries as signs of distress. Toddlers who grow under the watchful eyes of a teacher who understands how to arrange the environment for new walkers feel differently about themselves if their spirit of inquiry (aroused by something across the room, causing them to walk right on the hands of someone sitting nearby) is met with understanding about what just happened.

They understand that children's early experiences and attachments first affect their brain growth patterns and, later, their mobility, curiosity, spirit of adventure, and inquiry.

Yet as Stacie Goffin (2013, 40) comments in her book *Early Childhood Education for a New Era*, "Beyond societal changes and a more demanding political context, research studies document the field's inadequate performance, even as the knowledge base for informing effective practice has expanded." Clearly this is a discrepancy that needs to be addressed and an uncomfortable discussion that must take place in our field. Yet for many of us who have grappled with these issues for nearly a half century, frustration with the same old unresolved issues remains high. Goffin (2013, 40) goes on to say, "It is more possible than in the past to prepare skilled ECE teachers and thus more erroneous to ignore what is known." We know so much more than we did even a decade ago about how children learn. Yet we do little to demand application of this knowledge as it applies to teaching young children in group care.

14

What Society Expects of ECE Teachers

The discussion of theory and education is a difficult one for our field, and our approach to this discussion has often been to sacrifice quality to social expectations. During my CCR&R training sessions, many teachers demonstrated their lack of self-worth as professionals by prefacing their remarks with words like "I hate to say"; "I'm sorry to put it this way, but"; "It's embarrassing to admit"; "So many of us think this, but nobody ever wants to say it"; "We're not sure our director would understand, but"; "What point is there?" Their apologetic prefaces set the tone for whatever came next—the teachers first devalued their own ideas and words. It seems as though we don't value our role as professionals enough, or we mistake habit or conventional wisdom for core knowledge of the ECE profession.

The discussion of theory and education is a difficult one for our field, but it's also a difficult concept for the society we live in. And not just in the United States—Kate Ellis, who in 2013 was the Australian minister for early childhood, child care, and youth and minister for employment, was in the news for defending a bill (in her country) that would extend quality funds for teacher training and development to three hundred million dollars. This money would be spent solely for the purpose of educating and compensating early childhood workers in a more appropriate way. In her speech, she objected to politicians who call those caring for young children "dimwits." In other words, many people do not value our work. I was struck by similarities between Ellis's assessment of her country and my own experiences working in ECE. Ellis pointed out that many senior government administrators in Australia believe women should want to do ECE work out of the kindness of their hearts, "for the good of the children," without consideration of their need to be paid. This perspective is sometimes shared by women who choose to work with young children after their own children are grown or people who genuinely enjoy the many positives that come with spending time with growing children. We might enjoy riding in antique cars or looking at them in a museum. But such interest and enjoyment do not make us antique auto mechanics. And the same thing applies to teaching young children! The popular notion that the joy of being around young children is reward enough for taking positions in ECE or that pay and benefits are irrelevant to that joy does not do the field or the young children

The popular notion that the joy of being around young children is reward enough for taking positions in ECE or that pay and benefits are irrelevant to that joy does not do the field or the young children cared for any favors.

cared for any favors. It holds workers and children back from getting the best of what they need and deserve. And it continues to reinforce the popular notion that the work of caring for the next generation is not serious or professional work.

I quite agree with Kate Ellis that it needs to be a national priority in every country to designate money solely for the education of the ECE workforce. Families cannot manage the cost of quality care on their own—to pay wages worthy of quality ECE work requires government support, not unlike that used for educating children from kindergarten through high school. But too often the public doesn't understand or value ECE workers' training in foundational theories. Yet without it, we cannot provide or support quality child development in ECE.

Even more important than the general public's view of ECE is our own approach to the topic. In the earlier story, the teacher from the focus groups knew that the staff in her program were not equipped for the important work of nurturing babies and toddlers, but she felt powerless to do anything about it. Both Kate Ellis and the New Hampshire infant teacher acknowledged that the undereducated teachers were not stupid, but they lacked the appropriate educational background to do the work they were already engaged in. Both were rightfully offended by the disrespectful treatment of those caring for babies and toddlers. But both also acknowledge that these individuals needed more education to do the job as young children deserved to have it done. To address that problem, we need to take a look at the way we value—or don't value—a theoretical foundation in ECE work.

Far too often our attitudes toward early childhood education don't demonstrate care in our work, or our care for the connection between established theories and good practice. This manifests itself in the number of older Americans who have a "save-the-children" mentality regarding their work in child care. I have frequently heard my peer group say, "At least we cared enough to raise our own children. . . . We gave up things, but not our children's childhoods." It is hard for me to picture support for young families when the very caregivers of those families' young children do not respect those parents' need or desire to work, instead immediately casting a "bad parent" view on the families of the children they claim to care so much about. This is often done without malice, but the caregivers lack appropriate training in family support at the college level. More than ever, people working with young children and their families need education and understanding of child growth and development, ecological systems theory, sociology of the family, cultural sensitivity to poverty, and other environmental impacts. And salaries need to be raised to reflect this education.

Valuing and Understanding Our Work

Regional program coordinator for the NH CCR&R, Cindy Wallace, attended all the focus groups in our 2013 training. She agreed with the focus group participants who said they could

17

not get a bachelor's degree with the paycheck their child care work provided. Many participants also said they had colleagues who qualified for wonderful educational benefits, absolutely free, through the Child Development Bureau in New Hampshire, but they didn't want to make the time or the effort to take the courses. A seriousness of purpose is required to do an adequate job educating the next generation. It involves supporting families. It involves supporting colleagues and demanding the best from them. And it involves being lifelong learners ourselves.

The problems we face are overwhelming. Keeping a positive attitude is important, but also challenging, as we search for solutions. In the words of some child care practitioners who are also very committed teachers, "It's a negative for the field when people put so much energy into focusing on ECE not being respected rather than taking actions to gain that respect by continuing to grow and learn."

I agree with the observations these teachers brought to the table. I, too, have worked with people who just want to be left alone. They don't bring enthusiasm to the job. They are satisfied to use the same old lesson plans they created ten years ago. Some are not even looking for pay increases—they just want to maintain the status quo. ECE deserves more. "If you don't want to grow—it's time to go!" one of the participants wrote.

When I told Cindy Wallace about writing this book, she agreed with my frustration that the ECE workforce is not adequately educated to do this significant work . . . but she also countered that I offered no solution. "So why write this book; what do you hope to accomplish?" she asked. It was a good question without an easy answer.

I hope this book falls into the hands of some of those colleagues whom the focus group's participants described, or perhaps that it be pushed into the hands of those who complain about *both* lack of professional respect and salary *and* increased training requirements. *We can't have it both ways.* On the one hand, being a child care teacher is very demanding and important work. On the other hand, every profession that has struggled for respect and public acceptance of the importance of its work (nursing, for example) has had to accept that an increase in ongoing professional development precedes an increase in esteem. One of the teachers reflected these ideas best: "I'm ready to tell some of these people," she said, "if they don't care about learning about the ECE profession, its foundations, why what we do is important, they should go get a job doing something else that does not leave them responsible for educating young children. . . . If we want to teach, we need to continue to learn."

Chapter 2: Theories, Practices, and Their Foundations

WHEN I ASKED TEACHERS about their ideas on theory and practice, here are some of the things they said:

- Theories are what you learn about in college or workshops.

- Practices are what you do.

- Theories are what Piaget and Vygotsky wrote about.

- Theories are outdated for today's kids and teachers.

- Theories are about how you would like things to be, but practices are how it is every day.

- Theories are what the director makes you put in written plans.

- Practices are what you do all the time that sometimes has nothing to do with theory.

- Developmentally appropriate practice (DAP) is a theory. Fingerpainting and movement are practices.

- Constructivism is a theory. Constructing things in the classroom with clay or blocks or junk is practice.

- We are still "practicing" on our practices!

21

- Such a huge amount of time goes into eating, brushing teeth, toileting, resting, cleaning up, getting dressed and undressed, going outside, and waiting while everyone gets ready to do all of the above—those are all practices we engage in every day but don't usually think of as practice.

When I asked teachers to list one word to describe their daily practices with children, here are some of the words they used:

- teach
- learn
- support
- model
- observe
- guide

- nurture
- document
- communicate
- protect
- repeat
- plan

Working with the teachers who offered this information was a learning experience for me. Social and emotional development was stressed so much in the graduate program I attended many years ago that I have always believed that many of the richest lessons children learn at school and child care happen in the bathroom, at the lunch table, or when friends are arguing over the same toy. Yet the teachers I have worked with over the years (and many others, I imagine) didn't think of teeth brushing, toileting, napping, or sometimes even outdoor playtime as "curriculum practices." Even though teachers talked about practices as what they do all day, when discussion was stretched, they got back to things like math manipulatives or

I have always believed that many of the richest lessons children learn at school and child care happen in the bathroom, at the lunch table, or when friends are arguing over the same toy.

22

blocks or art experiences when defining curriculum, and lunch, nap, and getting dressed to go out as things that got in the way of their practices.

Based on the lists I compiled from these practitioners regarding theory and practice, it is clear that there is still a loud voice coming from the field stating:

- Theory is what you read.

- Practice is what you do.

- Theory is what the director wants in your lesson plans.

- Practice is what you actually do all day every day.

- Theory is how you'd like it to be.

- Practice is how it is.

Is Theory Really Relevant?

Comedian Rodney Dangerfield (1921–2004) made his reputation with his opening line, "I don't get no respect." Reviewing the previous comments of teachers about theory, it would seem theory is the Rodney Dangerfield of ECE's course of study. There are always jokes: "Yeah, well, in theory," "The theory is great, but try doing it with eighteen five-year-olds!" and "Yes, we are licensed for three- to six-year-olds, and yes, 'theoretically' they are all independently toileting, but, *of course*, we have a changing table!" Any experienced early educator has heard these and many other comments that point to a general disrespect for the relationship between theory and positive practices.

My many colleagues in Head Start have described the changes to their programs since the 2007 federal mandate for increased educational requirements for teaching staff. It is

23

It is clear to them that the more teachers know about theory and its implementation, the fewer struggles they have in their daily work with children.

clear to them that the more teachers know about theory and its implementation, the fewer struggles they have in their daily work with children. Easing one's own workload is not the first or most important reason for learning theory, though it does provide that beneficial motivation as well.

The range of child development theories available today is vast and includes many aspects of human behavior. It can be a challenge to beginners to know where to start. A good place to begin for the purposes of this book is with the word *theory*. Like many words in our language, it means a variety of things to people.

Often students will respond to theory as if it is opinion no different from their own. We frequently hear people say, "I have a theory about that." What they typically mean is that they have a hypothesis—a first attempt at explaining something. Having a hypothesis about something has been the initial spark of science and invention that leads to such amazing things as cures for polio, the electric lightbulb, computers, wireless phones, and Facebook and Twitter.

Thomas Edison didn't say I have a hypothesis one day and turn on the lights the next! For a hypothesis to become theory, it needs to be proven to be an accurate explanation over many attempts. Cures, inventions—and indeed, theories of child development—require days, weeks, or years of experimenting and testing the hypothesis. It is exemplary for a teacher to offer colleagues her hypothesis (she may call it a theory, but it is a hypothesis) that Jenny is not getting enough sleep lately because she keeps rubbing her eyes, is crying more frequently than usual, and is not getting along with her favorite friends. But the usual process would then be for colleagues to agree to observe Jenny more closely and talk with her family members to see if she has been getting enough sleep. This would be testing the teacher's hypothesis that Jenny's behavior and a lack of sleep are related. It would not, however, become a universal theory that children who cry frequently are tired based on this one child's behavior. The above hypothesis was developed by Jenny's teacher because she noticed something was wrong. This led her to watch Jenny more closely and later to develop the theory connected to fatigue because it made sense based on the facts she had as well as the frequency with which she observed the same facts. Sharing this with parents and other teachers in Jenny's life could provide the information needed to confirm or disprove the teacher's hypothesis. Even if she was right, her hypothesis would not become a theory until it had been *tested* over *time* on a large population of children.

Developing Theories from Research and Observation

The answer to the question "Where do our theories come from?" includes the following:

- data collected and organized from direct observations of young children

- data carefully analyzed to predict patterns of behavior

- observations of children drawn from their conversations or drawings

- testing the hypotheses of previous studies

- university-based studies

- government-based studies

- cross-cultural studies

- the work of professionals whose credentials in development, education, psychology, sociology, or medicine (or other related disciplines) lend credibility to our understanding of young children

- historic works such as Locke, Rousseau, and so forth that form the beginnings of child study

- resources from the National Association for the Education of Young Children (NAEYC), the Association of Childhood Education International (ACEI), and Zero to Three

When we are talking about the foundational theories of early childhood growth and development, we are talking about those ideas that have held up over decades or, in some cases, centuries. Or those ideas can be brand-new research based on careful observation and collection of data. In their book, *A Child's World*, Diane Papalia, Sally Olds, and Ruth Feldman explained it well years ago: "Theories are attempts to organize data, or information, in order to explain why certain events occur. A theory is a set of interrelated statements about a phenomenon. . . . Theories give us frameworks to help us make sense of our data, which we have obtained from scientific study. They let us go beyond isolated observations and come up with general statements about behavior. A good theory guides future research by being a rich source of hypotheses to be tested" (13–14).

It's important to acknowledge the difference between the personal hypotheses we might develop in our own classrooms drawn from a specific group of children and the theories considered as universal theories in the ECE field. In order to provide our best efforts for the children and families we work with, we need to bring both the documented research of the ECE field, as well as our own hypotheses, gleaned from observations and interactions to our daily work with them. When we work with and educate other people's children, we need to be able to think in universal and particular terms when making decisions that affect their well-being.

In order to provide our best efforts for the children and families we work with, we need to bring both the documented research of the ECE field, as well as our own hypotheses, gleaned from observations and interactions to our daily work with them.

An example of using theory to work with other people's children is adapting the sound policy of using real, child-size tools with children, as Maria Montessori has suggested. If we know that the parent of a child in preschool is anxious about a four-year-old cutting fruit with a real knife, we might do most of the cutting for this child (prior to setting the activity out), leaving just enough work that a plastic knife would do the job. When the child's fruit is presented, it looks the same as that of his or her friends. We are not making the decision to use plastic with everyone—instead, we are bringing individualization to our work and to this child by respecting the parent's wishes. Here we have generally adhered to sound ECE practice but made specific, appropriate adaptations for one child based on other issues. Yet, as in previous examples, our planning includes the universal base of knowledge accepted as foundational by the ECE field but is altered by common sense and what this child needs at this particular time and place.

The foundational theories in early childhood education are many. They are rooted in decades and, in some instances, centuries of child study and research. Some of these studies have been found less than adequate when applied to today's children and families. Some resonate as much today as when they were proposed by foundational theorists of our field—Montessori, Piaget, Vygotsky, and many others. Theorists look at human behavior through different lenses, and no one theory is universally accepted as *the* theory of how and why children grow and learn as they do. Many take an eclectic (basing ideas on a broad and diverse range of sources) approach to

The important goal is that, when teachers care about providing a quality experience for children, understanding the theories and growing with the theories of practice are necessary parts of their job.

child development theory. But the important goal is that when teachers care about providing a quality experience for children, understanding the theories and growing with the theories of practice are necessary parts of their job.

Also, knowing that respect for the body of knowledge our profession has called its own is essential for teachers. So is accepting Urie Bronfenbrenner's teachings that politics, media, culture, and community affect theory over time, changing its components. There are theorists whose work is not considered as relevant today as they were a century ago—for example, today's theorists believe that Sigmund Freud attributed more behavior to sexual repression than is actually the case. Another is pediatrician Benjamin Spock's counsel to leave infants to "cry it out" if we know they have been fed and have clean diapers. Despite their decreased relevance, these outdated theories can be helpful in understanding how we got to where we are today. It is similar to the reasons early childhood majors study the history of childhood, even though they no longer live in the Middle Ages or even the nineteenth century! Teachers need to stay current, read, reflect, and revise their positions as new research is presented, and they must accept that we need many approaches to address the needs of young children.

How We Use Theories in a Changing World

Observations and hypotheses become theory when valid means are used by those testing the hypothesis over time and observing the relationships between what children are doing and why. Research methods developed over years of study demand proof that they really work. Today we frequently hear of the need for evidence-based practices. This means that trials have been repeated over and over, leading to the same conclusions most of the time.

But research can always be questioned or added to, depending on situations and circumstances. For example, for decades educators have had concerns that research can be biased. And, indeed, some of it is. Perhaps most of us hear this in reference to standardized testing, which is not always an equally valid indicator for all children. Language, experience, and culture (to name a few variables) can affect research findings—or the lack of them. Critical thinking is important before we make decisions and apply them to the children we work with.

In classroom discussions of theory, students often hear that one researcher's ideas are not valid because the control group was too limited; another researcher is criticized because the group studied was not diverse or representative of children in child care. Piaget, for instance, has been criticized for doing much of his research using his own children. How do we know whom to believe when Piaget was very confident that children construct their own knowledge, while Vygotsky asserted that children are able to build much learning from their conversations with or observations of peers and teachers?

The twenty-first century offers such rapid change in almost every discipline that it can be a challenge to keep up; to compare; to know when to discard, when to adapt, and when to insist that something has withstood the test of time and is as valid as it was a century ago. Knowing more about the development of very young children today than we did even twenty-five years ago is exciting. Many things have contributed to this explosion in knowledge:

- Technological advances allow a larger percentage of the general public access to information.

- Greater numbers of children in the United States are spending many or some hours in group care, making more scientific child study possible.

- Media allow us to bring information about children, families, and education into the homes of anyone interested in these topics.

Access to all this information can be extremely positive and also quite overwhelming at the same time. A pregnant student in a child growth and development class once responded to my comment that when I was first pregnant in the 1960s, Benjamin Spock's *Baby and Child Care* was the only book on the bookstore shelf to help young parents prepare with a dramatic, "You don't know how lucky you were! You have no idea what it's like to walk into a bookstore, two months pregnant, and face three full aisles of books on parenting!"

I agree with this student: the abundance of reading material can be overwhelming. Early childhood educators who are caring for and educating other people's children need to keep ourselves informed, current, and curious about new trends. It's also a professional responsibility to both know and respect our field's knowledge base that has withstood the test of time. It is our job to carefully and thoughtfully weigh and observe new trends to determine if they inform and expand what we know about developing children. Just because a book has made it through the popular culture's requirements and found a place on commercial bookshelves does not mean it would pass examination in colleges or universities accredited to teach evidence-based practices that serve children and families well.

Early childhood educators who are caring for and educating other people's children need to keep ourselves informed, current, and curious about new trends.

There's really no excuse for not knowing current best practices. Today's technology allows us to access current, relevant, and necessary information quickly and easily. Resources such as Earlychildhood NEWS (www.earlychildhoodnews.com) and NAEYC's Position Statements (www.naeyc.org/positionstatements) can inform current promising practices in our field. These and other credible resources are valuable for students, teachers, parents, and others interested in learning more about young children's growth and behavior. It's important to note that finding information quickly online is very different from the years of study, observation of children, and supervised practice in ECE that students earning degrees in the subject are required to do. Ideally, for the professional early childhood educator, online resources are offered in addition to—not instead of—significant study of fundamental early childhood theory.

Another area receiving much attention today is the extent to which culture and community impact young children. We know that socioeconomic factors affect children's learning. We know that toxic stress and trauma-induced stress take their toll on children's ability to learn. We know that urban and rural living expose children to different strengths and

31

hazards. For example, children growing up in downtown Chicago are less likely to know the difference between deer and moose tracks than children growing up in northern New Hampshire. Children from extremely rural areas are not likely to understand public transportation, taxis, or Walk/Don't Walk signals. This does not mean some children are less competent than others, but instead that we need to remember context when studying trends and patterns. Then we need to alter our approach and materials to the particulars of individual children or a group's culture. This includes being realistic about the context in which we are attempting to share information. Teaching upper-middle-income children in a wealthy suburb demands different language and materials than teaching children who have had fewer experiences with books, music, or exposure to the natural world. The ECE profession has always acknowledged the importance of individualizing instruction. Recently, however, we have come to realize the extent to which, with an absence of malice, we took a more ethnocentric approach (judging another culture solely by the standards of one's own culture) to child development than was appropriate. It is exciting that we have grown in our capacity to recognize the importance of cultural competence and given more serious consideration to cultural and economic contexts.

The words we look for when considering foundational researched-based theory are *time-tested, respected methods of gathering data, context, science, peer review,* and *ability to translate outcomes to another population similar to the first.* Educators need to be open to change while respecting the time, context, and method of a theory's research. Working professionally with other people's children means acknowledging and respecting these important guidelines and methods so we can do our best for the next generation. Loving children and enjoying their company are as essential as knowledge of theories of child growth and development. Knowledge of theories of child growth and development is as essential to doing our best for children and families as loving children and enjoying their company. Both are necessary for continuous improvement in our work as early childhood educators.

The Practice of Our Theories

What are our practices? In the *Where We Stand* position paper on professional preparation standards, NAEYC is clear: "Excellent teachers are decision makers, engaged in a continuous interplay of theory, research, and practice" (2009, 1). Sadly, because many teachers are unfamiliar with ECE theories, many children in ECE programs are not exposed to practices based on foundational theories.

When we say *practice* in the context of ECE, we mean the planned activities we intend to offer to children throughout their days and years with us. These usually include curriculum areas such as mathematics, physical education, music, dance, science, literacy, and art adapted to the developmental ages and stages of the children we are teaching as well as their individual interests and abilities.

Practice also, however, means a way of responding to children during their days and years with us. Ideally, this way of responding includes consistent respect for children and their families, understanding their temperaments and individual preferences, understanding of their families' culture and preferences, and general knowledge of typical and atypical child growth and development.

Practice also, however, means a way of responding to children during their days and years with us.

Stating what our practices are or where they originated can be difficult because the field is so diverse and rapidly growing and because child care providers are not accountable in any real way to a single regulating office. In my state, for example, the Department of Health and Human Services (DHHS) regulates programs for children who are not yet in the public schools (in other words, in child care), while programs for children six and up (K–12 schools) are regulated by the Department of Education (DOE). This has always led to confusion for almost everyone involved. The past ten years have seen tremendous growth and collaboration between DHHS and DOE in planning for children of all ages.

Developing Our Practices

Our actions—indeed, our practices—as educators are informed by the kind of people we are, what we have learned, and where and how we have learned. Our practices come from the kind of people we have had as preschool and college teachers. Our practices come from our own temperaments—some of us are active, loud, exuberant, funny, and compassionate. Some of us are quiet, reflective, cautious, conservative, and compassionate. Some of us are young. Some of us are old. Some of us are rich, and some of us are not. Some of us are of North American or Western European descent. Some of us are Latino. Some of us are Irish. Some of us Nepali. Some of us are city dwellers. Some of us are not. Some of us have an extended family the size of a small state! Some of us have two living relatives. All of these factors affect what we bring to our work with children and families. And they should! We also need foundational theories to help us adapt the specifics of where we have come from to the needs and realities of the children we care for and teach.

We need to remind ourselves, as Lisa Delpit writes in her book *Other People's Children: Cultural Conflict in the Classroom* (2006), that there is a difference between educating our own and educating other people's children.

This is a complex job description. In my earlier discussions with teachers about theories versus practice, I loved the comment, "We are still practicing at our practices." This applies to teachers at every level, because to include all of these elements in one's approach to daily practice, a teacher needs thorough knowledge of theory through her quality postsecondary education, good mentors to help put the pieces together, excellent supervision, and time for reflection on all of these pieces, alone and in the company of coteachers.

Putting the Theories into Practice

When I reflect on my conversations with teachers, I am particularly struck by comments like "DAP is a theory but fingerpainting is a practice." For well-trained teachers who understand the foundational theories, *both* are *both*. Developmentally appropriate practice is a theory that becomes a practice, just as fingerpainting is a practice that is understood through theory. A well-informed and prepared teacher would say something like, "We have many children who have much to cope with in their very young lives, so we try to offer fingerpainting on a very regular basis. It is such a wonderful activity to relieve tension. We devote a good part of our budget each year to making sure we offer frequent and rich experiences with this medium."

This very brief description of the theoretical reasons for practicing fingerpainting with very young children tells us much about this teacher's understanding of both young children and of curriculum. Here are some things we know about her:

- She knows the children and families she is working with.

- She is aware of their stresses.

- She understands that coping skills are primitive in most three-year-olds and that they need appropriate outlets for their stress.

- She knows that finger-painting is both an art form (free, beautiful, interesting, and undefined) as well as therapeutic (a messy, tactile, squishy, direct sensory experience).

- She has learned that the experience is rich and relaxing when quantities and thickness of paint are carefully considered.

I could go on, but you understand the premise. This teacher is "practicing" DAP, and her knowledge of the children and the benefits of fingerpainting weave theory and practice together beautifully, making her work a fine example of what we can consider theories *of* practice. It is important to consider that such weaving of theories of practice requires knowledge and understanding of children, development, and curriculum. The above example does not separate theory (DAP) and practice (fingerpainting) but makes them one and the same.

It is important to consider that such weaving of theories of practice requires knowledge and understanding of children, development, and curriculum.

Now think of a teacher who does not understand the impact of stress on young children. She doesn't know any tension-relieving activities for young children or quality art experiences for young children. She sets out fingerpainting three times a

36

week because the director wants her to do so. This is an example of practice without accompanying theory.

As the studies cited earlier make clear, it is the ECE-specific training of the first teacher that makes the experience a quality experience for children. The first teacher is intentional in her choice for the children. She knows from her education that her planned activity is responding to particular children's needs. She would not urge all the children to paint—she would know that children in need would automatically choose to do it. The children who are not interested or don't like the feel of yucky paint on their fingers are free to make a different choice. The second teacher is doing as she is told. She sets out the activity three times a week, but that "task" could as easily be done by the custodian, the cook, or a parent volunteer. The challenge (and perhaps risk) in the second classroom is that the adults involved may not understand the intense need of some children for the activity or, equally as important, the need of other children to avoid the activity completely.

Theory-Informed Decisions: Adjusting Practices to Fit the Theory

It's always a bit of a challenge to speak seriously about theory. One of the reasons is that we often joke as if theories can't possibly work in real life. "Well, it works in theory!" we say, often followed by a few chuckles, implying that *it* is a whole other thing . . . and sometimes, that is absolutely true. In my many discussions with experienced teachers, all of them admit that, more often than they wish, their desired approach and their actual implementation of ideas are too far apart. I can relate. I have spent my entire career as an early educator split between direct service and teacher education/supervision of student teachers. The fact that I am well-schooled in the most appropriate techniques for working with and nurturing young children does not guarantee that I can always implement them in the way I'd like to or the way I believe is best for the young children in my care.

Let me share a recent example. During my last year as director of a program, I did story time after morning meeting with a group of more than twenty little ones. Most days it went okay. Some days it was wonderful. And sometimes colleagues would identify a child to help set up the next activity because they could see that story time just wasn't going to work for that child on that day. Because of my understanding of the theories, I do not believe in sharing books with very young children in very large groups. Why then did I do such a thing? Here are a few of the factors that led to my choice:

- We had an eleven-hour day.

- We tried to respect parents' difficulties in getting children to preschool on time each day.

- We had staggered staff schedules.

- The children and staff shared three large classrooms.

- The teacher who opened at six thirty needed a coffee before starting preschool.

- A quick meeting of all teachers about the morning before they got started benefited everyone.

- Morning meeting was in the middle room, where I did the story time and where late-arriving children entered. This allowed the other teachers to set up the other classrooms.

- I was one of the last staff to arrive, thus better able to "stretch" in doing what we would have preferred not to do.

- I am a pretty good storyteller, and most of the time it wasn't awful.

As a former children's literature instructor, I connect with the theories that suggest it's better to share stories one-on-one or with small groups of children. It is hard to select a book developmentally appropriate for a group ranging from young fours to six-year-olds. It is a challenge to have an interesting discussion when the group is so large that some children are always disappointed or act out because they didn't get to share their ideas.

I had to make many adjustments to this favorite activity of mine. It was a year when I was unable to share some of my favorite books because they simply wouldn't have worked with this size group. I took consolation in the knowledge that the children would all get a second chance at wonderful story times when they were in their smaller preschool groups. I made a point of selecting short books that were more enjoyable than thought provoking. I made a point of telling the children I could talk to them about the book at snacktime. And I left the book out all morning so when children had free time, they could take another look. It's not how I like to share children's literature with young children, but that last year it was the best I could do.

As I've experienced and as many teachers have told me: both theory and its applied practices need to be adapted to the realities of individual children and programs. Beyond that, practitioners often have to make adjustments to accommodate parents' or teachers' needs too. My story is an example of five educators making a decision that *this* year, with *these* children, arriving on *these* schedules, *this* was the best we could do. Our plan met the multiple needs of the children, families, and teachers *this* year. We made the collective decision to have a brief story time with an inappropriate group size. We believed that, *all things considered*, it was the best choice for everyone.

If we had decided that the parents were hopeless because they simply refused to cooperate by getting the children to the school by the requested hour every day, we would have had "too large" a group for story time based on sheer exasperation. Instead, we based our decision in part on accommodating parents' difficult schedules and their children's reluctance or inability to get going in the early morning. We were attempting to respond with empathy and support.

We could have based our decision solely on what we knew to be best (because we learned it through understanding theories) about quality book experiences for young children. We could have decided the group size was not to exceed eight children and that we would not compromise on quality. If we had made these decisions, that would have meant starting the day without teachers "touching base" with one another; with one teacher badly in need of a break as she headed into her preschool work; and with a strong measure of indifference to the families who tried but continued to arrive later than starting time. Each teacher could have planned her own quality book experiences for her own group (usually compatible in age and interests). This still would have left late-arriving children looking for their group and late-arriving parents feeling awkward because no one would have been available to talk to them if they needed or had information to provide. So our decision about having a large group size for story time was made and accepted by all because it was the best choice available at that point in time.

The important conclusion to this story is that because we understood the theories, we were able to make intentional decisions that adjusted our practices because of very specific and important program considerations. If a parent or student teacher were to ask anyone on the faculty why they were violating "best" practices (more on this later) with the group size, any one of us could have offered our rationale based on consensus about the challenges I've described. It remains a very different practice than if we didn't think about the quality of book experiences we were providing—but we knew the theory *and* we knew the children and their families, so our theories of practice were well and good.

The word *intentional* is critical to this discussion of theory and/of practice. *Intentional* in this case means that teachers have thought about what is being done and why. When teachers move beyond the position that there is only one "best" way to do things, they sharpen their skills at including sound theory in decisions about practice. Flexibility is also critical to both planning and supervising quality experiences for children. For instance, planning engaging curriculum in the outdoors is an important role for teachers. Setting up the outdoor environment for serious learning is part of our job. But sometimes experienced teachers know that children (for whatever reasons) just need to run and shout for a bit. Wise teachers shut down an inside activity that just isn't working and take the children with their high energy outside for some fresh air and exercise so they return with renewed interest to the task at hand. In this instance, the intentionality of the outdoor experience is purely physical and may have no intentional cognitive goals at all. It is not in the plan book! Yet it is clearly intentional teaching based on knowledge of the children's immediate needs.

Theories as a Foundation and Goal

I have mentioned so many considerations in implementing quality, appropriate, and meaningful practices in early education. There is a need to be intentional. There is a need to be informed. There is a need to be culturally and linguistically appropriate. We need to be humbly in awe of the many criteria we must consider and remember it is about the children and what is best for them.

Let's examine again that sentence from NAEYC's professional preparation standards: "Excellent teachers are decision makers, engaged in a continuous interplay of theory, research, and practice." I assume that it is not an accident that theory is mentioned first, followed by research, and finally practice in defining the decision making of excellent teachers. The evidence is clear and compelling: excellent teaching occurs when teachers learn the art and craft of teaching in quality professional preparation settings. Excellent teaching occurs when these teachers are then nurtured by continual and reflective supervision in environments where excellence is expected and continuous improvement is always a goal. Excellent teaching occurs when teachers have an understanding of foundational theory and a desire to implement it and when they continue to learn, study, and implement sound practices as part of their daily work with children.

Excellent teaching occurs when teachers have an understanding of foundational theory and a desire to implement it and when they continue to learn, study, and implement sound practices as part of their daily work with children.

Observation is one of the most important tools teachers of very young children use daily. Most degree programs in early childhood require at least a semester of course work and practice in observing and interpreting children's behavior. We develop skills at watching, listening, and trying to make sense of what individual children need at one point in time. Our observations inform how we respond to them. Our observations inform our decision, as described above, to redirect an activity because our knowledge of children is telling us the activity is not working today. If curriculum regularly comes from a written plan that teachers follow, even when it is not working, children lose. If children are not engaged, are too tired, or are disinterested, confused, angry, hungry, or any other number of things, yet we forge on because it is in the lesson plan, children lose.

The informed teacher, prepared with alternative ideas, can close the book that isn't working, put on some dancing music, and when the children are moving and laughing and on their own with the alternative, can settle on a sofa with Pedro and Heather, whose behavior shows her they really want to know how the story ends. This kind of teaching takes experience, willingness to learn from mistakes, a sense of humor, strong observational skills, courage, and knowledge of how children grow and learn. Without that foundational grounding in child development, many teachers don't know how to manage the daily practices, and this causes the behavioral breakdowns we hear so much about. Rather than investing all energy in ways to make children behave better, perhaps requiring investment in training that helps teachers redirect children's behavior and better meet and understand their needs would make more sense.

Chapter 3:
The Professional
Early Childhood Educator

UNTIL WE HAVE STUDIED and understand the theories that ECE is based on, they cannot be integrated into our daily practices with young children. There is a substantial body of knowledge that can unlock many of the secrets of why children act as they do. We know what we need to know . . . now the question is *how* do we learn it and support learning it?

Where Do We Stand as Professionals in ECE?

Unlike other fields of professional practice, ours is affected by many groups of people who think they know what to do with children based solely on the fact that they like them, have raised a few of their own, or have always had the ability to connect well with little ones. Though all of these factors contribute to the skills of those who work with young children and are very important, they alone are not adequate preparation for caring for and educating other people's children in group settings.

Stephanie Feeney has observed that whole contingents of workers who base their ideas on theories of conventional wisdom (a belief or set of beliefs that is widely accepted, especially one that may be questionable but popularly held as true) are employed in ECE workplaces (Feeney 2012).

Others, such as Stanford University's Center for Education Policy Analysis, have noted that many involved in the ECE

45

workforce do not have postsecondary education or degrees in early childhood growth and development or education (Bassok et al. 2013). When discussing these findings with my colleagues, I was surprised by their sense that we had made more progress in this area in the last twenty-five years than the research findings indicate. I believe the reason for this stems from the number of colleagues whose work in state government, higher education, or Head Start involves them with programs whose standards are monitored at a higher level than most programs for children under the age of five generally are.

In programs with lower levels of monitoring, the people who work with and care for children are often not paid a living wage. Their salaries do not make it possible for them to continue their education (Smith and Baughman 2007). Often the ECE workforce does not want to admit the relationship between low wages and a lack of adequate professional preparation. So long as we do not require more advanced study of those working with very young children, their salaries will remain static. We are caught in a vicious web of people needing more education but not being able to afford it.

Evidence for Theory-Based Education

We are not in the dark when it comes to the criteria leading to quality care. Beginning with the National Day Care Study in 1979 (followed by many credible studies that concur with those findings—for example, Feeney 2012 and Goffin 2013), studies have made it clear that a few very specific things are common to most programs offering quality care:

- small group size

- low ratios of adult caregivers to children

- early childhood–specific education of caregivers

The fact that these findings have been repeatedly duplicated surely suggests that early childhood–*specific* education is a huge predictor of a quality program.

For many years, when posting desirable jobs, I worded my search to include "ECE training and experience required." Initially, support staff asked if I thought I should write out what ECE stood for. My answer was always no. I was not looking for candidates who didn't know what ECE stood for. Additionally, I would quickly hire a candidate with an associate degree in ECE over applicants with a master's degree in anything else. Knowing how children grow and react to a variety of circumstances is critical to adequately nurturing their learning and development.

It is necessary to address the discrepancy in the ECE field between the knowledge that early childhood–specific education is an indicator of quality programming and accepting the fact that many in the field continue to avoid requiring that education of the workforce. It is like the five-hundred-pound gorilla in the room that no one mentions. We need to have more frequent, honest, and respectful conversations about our differences of opinion on this subject. In chapter 2, I made the point that loving and enjoying children is essential to working with them, and professional training is equally important. Too often our field has used an either/or rather than a both/and when looking at teacher credentials. Educator Herbert Kohl was right thirty years ago when he wrote, "With the rarest of exceptions, one has to learn how to become a good teacher just as one has to learn how to become a scientist or an artist" (1984, 16). Teaching is a learned art, and we must recognize it as such within our field.

Teaching is a learned art, and we must recognize it as such within our field.

47

Thirty years ago, the child care system was not as developed as it is today. More recent research on children's early brain development has done much to convince ECE professionals that developmental needs must be taken seriously from conception on. Infant and toddler care is as important if not more important than the care and teaching of three- and four-year-olds during their preschool years. Yet frequently the general public is unaware of the critical learning that takes place all day every day for young children. This lack of understanding is so widespread that it reaches right into the ECE workplace. Many directors have told me that, like me, they have difficulty staffing the infant room because staff say they want to "really" teach.

Daphna Bossok and her colleagues claim, "The few studies that have examined the evolution of the ECE workforce over time actually suggest that the qualifications of the workforce have either changed only modestly or have declined" (2013, 583). If average child care employees have only high school diplomas or, at best, associate's degrees, they are unlikely to possess the know-how to create the learning environment or experiences for children provided in public school pre-K or kindergartens, where teachers have a degree in early childhood education and are certified teachers. This does not necessarily mean the child care center is poor quality or the providers are bad people, but years of data tell us that we will recognize the difference when we walk into those two classrooms. For the good of all of our children, *we need more people with child development and education degrees teaching and caring for young children.*

Even knowing how the level of teacher training affects the quality of education and care for young children, following the excellent guidelines for practice provided by NAEYC, ACEI, and Zero to Three is not required of any accredited programs. There is a gap between what we know is best for children and what we are able to provide, given the lack of appropriate funding structures and differences of opinion about how to manage the dilemma of quality, cost, and affordability.

In her speech to the Australian Parliament mentioned earlier, Ellis pointed out that ECE staff qualifications and training is the number one indicator in Australia of quality programs for children. That has also long been the case in this country (Ruopp et al. 1979). Ellis stated that bachelor's degrees are the necessary preparation to work with young children. She mentioned the "ignorant misunderstandings" (of those who oppose funding adequate salaries) in the face of compelling evidence about what our children need and deserve. It is the same issue we need to address in this country if we are to honestly face the question of how to supply and pay for the teaching requirements needed to provide children with quality early education. When large numbers of the ECE workforce have no training past high school, how do we hope for them to merge our foundational theories with their daily practices?

Let me share an example. A colleague who was at the time an ECE professor tells the story of a student in her curriculum class. The college had accepted the student without required prerequisites, and when the professor discussed the use of concrete materials when teaching very young children math concepts, she was interrupted by the new student. The student sincerely stated that maybe concrete materials were better than writing numbers on paper, but she thought it was wrong to make tiny children use things made from cement because they are just too heavy for little ones. The professor kindly explained that in ECE, concrete materials are things children can hold in their hands, move around, or touch, because holding mathematical concepts in their minds is too hard for little children.

When large numbers of the ECE workforce have no training past high school, how do we hope for them to merge our foundational theories with their daily practices?

49

Teachers need to be familiar with educational terms and the theories before they can practice them. If aspiring early educators do not understand the need to learn about these foundational theories or their relevance to daily practices with young children and their families and pursue them with seriousness of purpose, then possibly they should pursue other lines of work. If aspiring ECE educators cannot afford to go to school, then it is in the best interest of our children for this funding to be found and provided.

It is important to note here that it is quite possible for teachers to go through the process of getting a degree in ECE and still not make the necessary connections between theory and practice. My graduate school supervisor used to say, "There are, of course, students who go through the program, but the program never quite goes through them." I find that those who oppose college requirements for ECE teachers tend to frequently use the rationale that just because someone goes to college doesn't guarantee that she or he will be a good teacher. That, of course, is true. Research, however, demonstrates that the odds of becoming a good teacher are greatly increased by rigorous training in both child development and early education (Ruopp et al. 1979). It's also the case that teachers can study child development yet not apply this knowledge in their work with children. However, if teachers haven't studied it at all, then it is luck or coincidence if they manage to make the best choices for children and their early education. Children deserve better.

Addressing Sticky Topics and Standing Up for Our Own Profession

Pondering our complex professional dilemmas requires reflection, honesty, and flexibility. Another participant in one of the ECE focus groups I worked with claimed that the diverse challenges teachers face are often not met because reflection, honesty, and flexibility are not the top skills of many early education practitioners. "We are so good at understanding the uniqueness and individual needs of young children and so bad at recognizing and dealing with [the individual needs] with each other!" she said. It is time for many of us in the ECE field to ask ourselves why we don't respect each other and the work we do with children.

When this teacher described the prevalent trait among early educators of accepting uniqueness and difference in children but not in our coworkers, other teachers twisted uncomfortably in their chairs. I observed exactly what others have noted and described: In her provocative book *Early Childhood Education for a New Era: Leading for Our Profession*, Stacie Goffin rightly quotes Sue Bredekamp: "The barrier of attitudes among early childhood professionals seems to be the hardest to talk about, the most divisive, and perhaps the one that most strongly thwarts our efforts for change" (2013, 40). There was a measurable discomfort in the room, and many faces registered the deer-in-the-headlights look that prefaces the groans and "Oh, let's not even go there" that I've heard when such discussions provoke discomfort. The conversation was avoided that evening, much to the relief of many participants.

It seems so curious to me that proposing we have more respect for one another should trigger such avoidance. Yet I have seen it over and over in the past forty years at child care association and directors' meetings. People seem to understand that with more respect comes higher pay, and sometimes the groans are from directors who know they haven't the budget to pay higher wages. The groans are also heard from very experienced child care providers who came in the back door of the field (volunteering at their own child's program, for instance, and then filling an emergency vacancy), have worked their way up, and

51

prefer the status quo to going back to school. Sometimes it's the young teacher who is still paying for an associate's degree and grimaces when leadership discusses raising the bar to bachelor's level entry requirements.

All of this groaning, in my estimation, stems from the fact that what is good for many current workers in the ECE field and what is best for the education and care of young children differ. That difference can only be resolved by recognizing the conflicting needs within the existing workforce: the need of the undereducated person already employed working with children to keep her job versus the need of the well-educated person looking for a well-paying job teaching children. We will not make progress as a field until we address these conflicting needs head-on.

Here's how it boils down for me: I would not begin to question the knowledge mothers pick up while raising children. Unquestionably, mothers can pick up insights about children that a doctorate in child growth and development does not provide. Frequently teachers tell parents that they (the parents) are the "experts" when it comes to their own children. This is often true. However, as Lisa Delpit (2006) points out, this does not make parents experts when it comes to other people's children. To manage the needs of other people's children professionally requires a far broader knowledge of education and development, individual and group culture, and individual and group learning processes. This tension between natural insights and formal education has been the primary point of conflict in the ECE field for as long as I can remember.

To manage the needs of other people's children professionally requires a far broader knowledge of education and development, individual and group culture, and individual and group learning processes.

The well-educated and trained teachers have learned and can integrate many theories into their daily practices. It takes years

52

of study and commitment to the importance of this work to do our best for the children and families we work with. Unlike most professions, however, the admiration or acknowledgment of our colleagues for the years put into advanced studies are often denigrated rather than applauded. Determining why this is so is a complex and delicate matter and thus a topic frequently avoided. But avoidance benefits no one. Therefore, I am hopeful that opening general discussion within the ranks of early childhood workers at all levels can help us learn from each other, listen to each other, and move the discussion forward. I think it is important for those who think degrees are unnecessary preparation for working with young children to articulate the reasons behind their belief. I think it is equally important for those of us who believe we must raise the bar on education and training in ECE to articulate the reasons behind our thinking. I encourage believers in both perspectives to engage others in the workplace in open and respectful discussion.

Many people talk about how ridiculous it is to train people (typically women) to work with young children when women have been doing this since the beginning of time. And many child care teachers resent a pay scale that includes level of education as well as years of experience when computing compensation. We don't like to talk about it that much, but we know that this discussion goes on in staff rooms, outside play areas, and at off-hours social gatherings of people who work together. It is possible to hear the very same people complain of low wages, long hours, and increased training requirements. Yet in most professions, compensation, hours, advancement, and titles are linked to specialized training and coursework.

As Stephanie Feeney (2012) points out, standards for licensing and program standards vary greatly from state to state. Federally funded, NAEYC-accredited programs, university-based programs, and Head Start programs have stricter requirements and higher levels of accountability than programs that are funded solely by parent tuition. Until very recently, Feeney (2012) writes, ECE was seen as a service for working families rather than for educating our young children.

I believe this historic perspective of caring for children is also the reason that one frequently hears the justification for an untrained workforce as the knowledge that kind, sensitive, loving caregivers provide children what they truly need. It is true that young children need adults in their lives who are kind, sensitive, and loving. But it is also true that kind, loving, sensitive adults who do not know and understand the developmental needs of young children and the expected behaviors and strategies for supporting growth at various stages of development can only do *half of the job*. Let me stress that this can also be said of the teacher with a master's degree in ECE who lacks warmth and genuine enjoyment of very young children. In either of these cases, children are getting half of what they need.

Anti–higher education attitudes are clearly not a factor everywhere within our field, but it is my bet that most ECE professionals recognize some of their own professional networks in the scenarios described above. Those who teach teachers have probably experienced at least a few student teachers who return from field experiences where they have been told by teachers at the site that "all that theoretical junk won't matter when you get out here!"

It is to the credit of our profession and the work of Sue Bredekamp and Carol Copple that *Developmentally Appropriate Practice* (DAP) is now in its third edition. What prevents ECE from moving forward is the fact that all over the country, children are cared for up to eleven hours a day by caregivers who have not read the DAP book. If providers have had no exposure to the importance of DAP, they can't know the difference developmentally appropriate practices might make in their daily work with children and families.

I was happy to have a conversation recently with Ellen Wheatley, the child care administrator of New Hampshire, who admitted that though we need to be open to many ways of educating our workforce, part of the message is that *our workforce needs to be educated*. The world is constantly changing. What we know about children and their learning and growing constantly grows and changes. Early educators need to have a set of skills and abilities that include a commitment to lifelong learning (Wheatley, pers. comm., July 2013).

Early Childhood Educators as Professionals— What Does It Look Like?

So if we are going to have these conversations, as I hope we will, one question at the top of the list is "What does it mean to be a professional in ECE?" Here are thoughts from others in the field in answer to this question. I hope they will inspire you to engage with your colleagues.

"Teachers are teachers because they have studied education and children. We just need to do it. We need to require degrees of those who teach children in these formative years" (Dean Tessa McDonnell, Granite State College, pers. comm., July 2013).

"In complex, modern societies responsibility for different aspects of people's welfare is assigned to specialized experts who are called professionals. These people provide something that is viewed as critical to the overall well-being of the members of a society. Not only do professionals provide a significant service but they are also, *because of their training*, the only ones who are equipped to provide this service" (Feeney 2012, 6, emphasis mine).

55

Feeney (2012) writes that the professional's expertise comes from a high level of generalized and specialized knowledge. This is where theory comes in. ECE theory is the specialized knowledge Feeney refers to. I have met few professionals with graduate degrees in ECE who aren't able to quickly connect Vygotsky to ZPD (zone of proximal development) or Dewey to progressive education. These are some of the foundational theories of our practices. Yet as I described in chapter 1, I have worked with groups of experienced educators who could not connect the basic theories of our profession with their founding philosophers. Of even more concern to me is that many of those educators did not find that fact upsetting. I have spent many years working with and talking about this issue with practitioners and know that this lack of concern is not unusual.

At our national conferences, the issue of ECE being a profession has been a hot topic of debate for decades. Kyra Ostendorf, executive editor at Redleaf Press, noted as recently as the NAEYC Institute for Professional Development conference in Minneapolis (2014), attendees discussed the need for direction in teaching standards (Ostendorf, pers. comm. 2014). I remember a NAEYC national conference thirty years or so ago where a panel of senior professors spoke on the state of the field. Several offered enthusiasm about the increased attendance. Others spoke with enthusiasm about the Harvard Preschool Project. James Hymes concluded the session by saying something to the effect that he guessed somebody had to rain on the parade and be honest: higher education and the Harvard Preschool Project were just grand and helpful, but all over the country, working families had to leave their children in the care of individuals with no understanding of young children at all. What's more, he continued, most people seem to think that's just fine, including the folks sitting in this room! The hall fell silent, the session was complete, but I heard participants criticizing his words as they left the room. "How can a negative attitude like that help anything?" one woman said.

This story reminds me of a program director who left a seminar on standards after listening to colleagues discuss an article in the *Nation* about the deaths in a Texas family child care home. "This is horrific and negative," she said. "This is not who we are!" She was right that those attending the six-hour seminar on a beautiful summer day cared passionately about their work with children and their own continuing education. But to refuse to look at the conditions that are harmful to children does not serve our field well. It also leaves too many children in harm's way. Children deserve better, and so does our field.

Undeniably, early childhood educators face challenges to professionalism: the public believes itself to be just as informed about what works for children as ECE professionals. (This is not the case for attorneys, CPAs, physicians, engineers, or architects, whose specialized skills and knowledge are often accepted, without question, by those seeking their services.) The ECE field has for years extended professional

> *Undeniably, early childhood educators face challenges to professionalism: the public believes itself to be just as informed about what works for children as ECE professionals.*

titles to workers whose status at best could be described as paraprofessional. We want to be inclusive. We have already set the precedent of pushing for this professional status, and we don't quite know what to do with the dilemma we are in.

Yet we remain in the pattern Gwen Morgan (1986) called the "trilemma" of early childhood services. If ECE is to meet the needs of clients, it must have quality, availability, and affordability. (In ECE, quality is understood as meaning a program that employs teachers with ECE-specific training.) We cannot seem to combine the three. We have sacrificed quality to affordability, accepting compensation that does not cover the cost of providing bachelor's degree–trained, credentialed teachers to all of our children, supported by paraprofessionals who can make careers of supporting teachers' work or go back to school to become teachers themselves.

Having Cake and Eating It: What Professionalism Means for ECE

Too many ECE workers calling themselves professionals rail against increased standards and professional development. This needs to change. When providers struggle with low pay, few benefits, and little job prestige—yet resist the kind of activity that has moved other workers (nurses, for instance) from the world of paraprofessionals to the world of adequate pay, benefits, and job satisfaction—they are holding the entire field back.

Typically, when discussing standards and wages, the ECE field has responded with unsuccessful attempts to solve the problem or to make this issue of professionalizing the field go away. In the past, we have often responded to this problem with these approaches:

- inclusiveness for all staff working with children (Everyone is labeled a teacher regardless of qualifications.)

- reliance on conventional wisdom (If you've raised children, you can teach them.)

- avoiding the wages issue (We can't do anything about it, so why bother to change it?)

The problem is that none of these responses serves our profession in a way we would like. Each of these approaches has caused its own set of problems and does not resolve them.

Inclusiveness for All Staff: Too Much of a Good Thing

Feeney quotes educational leader John Goodlad, "A vocation is not a profession just because those in it choose to call it one" (2012, 17). This clearly applies to the complex and complicated nature of the ECE workforce. With the best intentions, many early educators insisted years ago that everyone in the building working with children be called a teacher. The rationale behind that decision was one of inclusion. It seemed like a good idea at the time. But now, reviewing newer thinking about ECE professionals and the meaning of a "profession," many in the field realize that specialized training is needed to be accepted as true professionals. Feeney's book is a fine read for those interested in why this is so.

Conventional Wisdom: Experience Isn't Enough for Other People's Children

There is ongoing conversation from both directors and the "teachers" they hire who defend a "teacher's" superior abilities based solely on years of parenting or working with young children. "I have experience," some workers say proudly. (As well they should . . . combined with serious study and practiced skills.) Often they add that those college girls haven't got any ideas about discipline—they just want to read "quality children's books." When I reflect on the word *experience*, I have to acknowledge that it is quite possible to have thirty years of experience at doing something poorly; experience alone does not make a qualified professional. This is not to say that there are not wonderful individuals working with young children who do not have adequate, ECE-specific education and are nonetheless doing a fine job. There are! But research since 1979 has repeatedly indicated that these special teachers with no educational training in ECE are not as abundant as conventional wisdom would have us believe (Ruopp et al. 1979). Keeping this view alive, however, is convenient because it protects us from having to take the complicated step of actually requiring appropriate training and compensation for those who care for and educate our children.

Sitting in appropriate training is not enough. As stated previously, my supervisor in graduate school would occasionally make the comment, "You know we've had some people go through this program that obviously just never had the program go through them!" It's not that we can't find examples of well-educated, unqualified teachers, but well-documented research says they are rare. Yet those hoping to maintain the status quo use them repeatedly. I state confidently that no matter how many times we choose to say, "She is a natural-born teacher and she never went to college," or "He has a master's in ECE but he has no idea how to act with children," that *most of the time this is not the case*. Nearly forty years of research has repeatedly and consistently found that those with early childhood–specific education create programs of better quality than those led by the conventional wisdom so many of us want to rely on (Whitebook 1990).

Both parenting and teaching behaviors are greatly affected by how much we really know about children's behaviors. Conventional wisdom, however, holds out for "maternal instinct" and "born" teachers. It is my hope that discussion of this manual will prompt caregivers, providers, parents, teachers, and anyone else involved with the care and education of the very young to reflect on the extent to which both parenting and teaching are roles that evolve with experience and education. I believe that conventional wisdom describes how most people view competence in nurturing the young. It is widely accepted that most women are born knowing what children need and how to deliver that. Compelling research as well as anecdotal stories and popular literature defy this notion. In *Blue Nights*, one of novelist Joan Didion's characters says, "I do not know many people who think they have succeeded as parents" (2012, 93). I agree with her. Many of us, if our child-rearing years are over, have come to peace within ourselves that we did the best we could at the time. But few of us are entirely free of regrets.

The same is true for many of us as educators. Ideally, we get better with years of experience. We learn more through continued education. We draw insights from colleagues. We take time to reflect on our experiences in the classroom and revise our approach or lesson plan. We also have regrets. We remember the child we tried so hard to help but failed. We regret the instances when we did a less than adequate job and could have done better "if we knew then what we know now!"

In both parenting and teaching, the importance of reflection, learning, ability to forgive ourselves for less than adequate performance at times, restructuring our frame of mind, and changing our own behavior over time will improve our interactions with children. It is not the goal of this book to outline differences between parents' and teachers' behavior. I want to emphasize, however, that we all need to explore this area if we work with young children. Rights, responsibilities, and appropriate boundaries are all woven into the difference in these two roles. Lilian Katz (1977) in *Talks with Teachers: Reflections on Early Childhood Education* has provided much information about why and how parents' and teachers' roles are and should be different. I recommend this book to all of those unfamiliar with Katz's work on teacher and parent roles. I reference Katz's work on parent/teacher similarities and differences because both roles have been formed and reformed over the years largely by conventional wisdom.

One of the critical ways the behaviors of both teachers and parents need to be the same is in maintaining a good sense of humor. We need to laugh at our own folly, laugh at well-laid

61

plans that go awry, laugh at our hopes of keeping everything on track the day of the field trip, and make the most of all of the above anyway. Working with and raising young children is delightful but hard work. Contexts, conditions, and knowledge are always in motion. Keeping up with it all to do our best for the next generation is never easy.

But Who Will Pay for It? Avoiding the Wages Issue

Often teachers work at the mall at night because they need new tires or food and can't afford to live on the wages they earn caring for children. I continually hear them discuss this and find it immensely discouraging. I believe that most wages in ECE do little to inspire young adults to make it a career. So where do we go from here?

When sharing many of the ideas raised in this book with colleagues, I've learned that a frequent concern they have is that restructuring the workforce would leave many people currently working in the field out of a job. It does not have to be that way. For any such restructuring to take place, there would have to be short- and long-range planning. An example is the Head Start Act 2007 mandate, which states that 50 percent of the Head Start workforce must have bachelor's degrees by the year 2014. This indeed is exactly what Head Start has done. I spoke with Pat Meattey, Educational Coordinator for Strafford County Head Start, New Hampshire, about implementation of this mandate. She has been with her agency for twenty-eight years and so has a good grasp of services delivered before, during, and after this transition. I asked her one question . . . with two parts! "Was the transition difficult, and has it made a difference?" Her response was as follows:

- Absolutely—to both!

- I see far more intentional teaching today.

62

- Teachers have the ability to articulate why they are doing what they do.

- Teachers are more competent to withstand the current pressures for academics and accountability.

- Teachers use more preventive strategies and are far less reactive than previous teachers without degrees.

- The bachelor's level teachers understand visual cues, reinforcement, and a variety of strategies.

- They are active problem solvers.

As all of us in ECE know, the topic that staff discuss over and over is children's behaviors. Meattey reports that this area stands out in her mind as the primary difference between well-trained professional staff and those with good intentions but no significant education in child growth and development. She remembers twenty years ago when staff would pounce on children for what they considered misbehavior. Today the well-educated teachers look for reasons for children's behavior. They analyze it and try to determine ways they can adapt the environment or change the curriculum to better meet the needs of particular children. Instead of trying to change them, they focus on trying to change their approach to the children. At a time when many say behaviors are continually getting worse, the Head Start programs, now staffed with at least 50 percent of teachers who possess strong, theory-based knowledge of children, are seeing fewer incidents of extreme behaviors. Meattey attributes this not to changes in the children's behaviors but to the prevention strategies and reactions of well-trained professionals.

Instead of trying to change them, they focus on trying to change their approach to the children.

Most of the teachers I speak with who continue their education (even though it is time-consuming and sometimes expensive) admit, in retrospect, how much easier advanced training has made their job because they have learned what works at what ages, what behavior is typical at certain ages, and how to be proactive rather than reactive when supporting children's growth and development.

Change Requires Real Work

Returning to my initial point about the separation of theory *and* practice, one has to ask, how has this separation occurred? When theory is taught without a context, it is very difficult for students to think about. The profession has made great strides in its attempts to offer accessible training at a variety of levels. There's a wide array of textbooks that are more direct and offer examples of applying theory to classrooms. Yet many practitioners continue to describe theory as *coursework* and practice as *daily work*. So why is this so? When I look back from the National Day Care Study and proceed to Marcy Whitebook's most recent work, the answer is the basic premise of this book: you can't practice theory if you don't know it. Given that roughly half of our field doesn't know it, how can we expect them to practice it? We can't!

It's like the expression, "If you do what you've always done, you'll get what you've got!" Our field has known for years that there is a connection between how adults treat children and how children behave. We have known for many years that quality education and care for children is far more likely when the adults who share their days have college-level training in child growth and development (Ruopp et al. 1977). Yet, in many instances, we have continued to allow individuals who have never studied how children grow and learn to become their earliest teachers and caregivers.

We know that to do our best for our children, our field needs to change. We need to do something different. But most of us don't like change. It takes hard work. It isn't easy. We want the change, but we don't want to have to work so hard to get it. There will be conflict, disappointment, mistakes, trying to learn from the mistakes—all those things we'd like to avoid. So we do what we've done, and we get what we've had . . . even though we admit our children deserve better.

I believe most of us don't want to maintain the system that we currently work within. Our differences lie in what we think could change it. Here are some of the solutions I've heard at conferences and by talking to people (both ECE workers and the public):

- The government should fund programs from birth through college.

- We need to have more quality in higher ed programs for teachers.

- Parents need to do a better job.

- Children should behave the way they used to.

- Teachers should have degrees.

- If ECE people were paid more, maybe they would do a better job.

- Make teachers more accountable.

- Create policy at the Department of Education, NAEYC, or ACEI that everyone in every state has to follow.

- If families stayed home until their children were in first grade, we wouldn't have the problem.

From this list, I pulled some that seem more relevant to ECE than others:

- We need improved college programs for early educators.

- Teachers need ECE degrees to have the tools they need for their work.

- A unified policy expected of early educators throughout the country with accountability to one entity might help.

It seems to me, in looking at these three items, that much work and understanding of these facts already exist:

- Much effort has gone into early childhood program planning at the college level.

- Research has established and professional practitioners agree that ECE degrees are necessary to give teachers of young children the tools that best work with children.

- NAEYC has provided excellent guidance (generally accepted by most ECE professionals and institutions) on DAP for children, birth to age eight. These are present in quick, easy-to-read form for the very busy and in more extended form for those wanting more. (For concise information on DAP, Code of Ethics, and ECE resources, see Feeney 2012.)

To a great extent, our challenge is not really any of the above. Our challenge is to take the leap (as Head Start did in 2007) of requiring the necessary work of prospective early childhood educators to prepare them for meeting the needs of our country's young children.

We want to hold up the examples of wonderful women who have nurtured generations of other people's children without ever going to college. And these women exist, just as the women who have been granted a graduate degree in ECE, but just really don't enjoy children that much and bring less than children deserve when they arrive at work in the morning. More work to counsel both of these extremes needs to be done. To support the first group of well-intentioned but undereducated staff, incentives for additional workshops and training could be offered. In the latter case, supporting someone in making another career choice may be the only option. As I can best read the studies, both of these are the exceptions to the rule. But if all of us were more open to frank and respectful discussion, we might generate more plentiful solutions.

Mostly the people who bring what children need with them to work in the morning are those who have a passionate love of children, a bachelor's degree in ECE or other early childhood-related disciplines (such as pediatric nursing, child and family studies, or sociology of families), and a true enjoyment of spending time with young children. And sometimes these develop with time and experience! It is important to add that large programs often have many positions for loving adults without ECE degrees. They can work as aides, volunteers, floaters, and assistant teachers *under the supervision* of adequately trained professionals. It is when these workers are left alone in classrooms, without supervision, that we do them and the children they care for a disservice.

It is, perhaps, time for more of us who know that outstanding practices with children cannot happen in the absence of teachers' understanding of theoretical foundations to say so out loud.

This is not always a popular stand to take. If current research is correct in stating that the majority of our workforce does not have adequate, ECE-specific education and teacher training, we might want to try putting more energy into increasing our expectations for early childhood teachers rather than trying to make the most of the existing workforce when we know they lack the necessary foundational work.

I have spent months—decades, really—trying to find a different answer to the question "How do we unify theory and practice?" other than requiring that all teachers go to school and commit to memory—and understand—the basic foundational theories of the field in the context of daily work with children. I haven't come up with a better answer.

Once a student and later an employee of mine asked me how I remembered all of these theorists and what they did and what it meant. I know I disappointed her, and will disappoint readers, by my answer: "I memorized them," I told her. "It's my job to know all of this." I recited what I was trying to learn into a cassette player (all that was available when I began my career) and played it in the laundry room when folding laundry, played it in the kitchen when fixing dinner, and played it on my hour commute to the university, where I was working on my master's in ECE. I was young at the time, so teaching kindergarten and raising three young children of my own seemed little reason to hold me back from continuing to work at learning more about these five-year-olds whose words and actions kept me continually perplexed. So I took out loans, unsure if future income would pay them back.

Decades later I could, perhaps, question my judgment for teaching all morning and then driving an hour each way to be a student at the university. I can question the soundness of borrowing against an uncertain future. But I also applaud myself for the passion I brought to the situation. I can admire my self-assessment that I did not know enough about young children to be spending many hours nurturing and educating them. I wanted to be a better mother and teacher, and no one had prepared me for either job.

The payoff on this investment came sooner than I thought. I found that teaching and mothering were getting easier. The more I learned about child growth and development, the easier it was at work and at home. This bears repeating: *the more we know about child growth and development, the easier daily work with children becomes.*

The more I learned about child growth and development, the easier it was at work and at home.

The more we know about children, the easier it becomes to cope with their developmental storms, their temperamental challenges, and their unique and idiosyncratic behaviors. Notice that I say it becomes *easier,* not that it becomes *easy.* There are no easy answers. Working with children is very demanding. If they are your own children, there are many things involved besides knowing about children in general. But the knowledge of typical behaviors can ease the stress one feels regarding ages and stages that are just plain difficult to get through. It can be as easy as having confidence to know that "this, too, shall pass!" It can help us to know when to acknowledge that this isn't going to pass, and we'd best get help from someone else. It is win-win for all and the greatest investment in the future I can imagine.

Many of us know from surveys by the Child Development Bureau and CCR&R that the most frequently requested training by practitioners is "Guiding the Behavior of Young Children." As long ago as twenty-five years, when I would teach this course for my university system, it was clear to me that most teachers or parents taking the course wanted children to do what they said. They were not that interested in learning active listening skills or strategies and frameworks for asking questions ("Would

69

you like tuna or chicken?" instead of "What would you like for lunch?"). Often they resisted my suggestion that they not offer a choice when there really wasn't one ("Would you like to go out?" rather than "We are going out. Do you want to put on your jacket or shall I help you?"). In other words, I was suggesting that they change, try new strategies, and refine new skills, when what they really wanted was to come to a class where someone would tell them how to make the children behave! The point is that frequently we all want easy answers to hard questions. But too often we hesitate to invest the time and energy to get the outcomes we desire.

When we talk about joining theory and practice into a single function—the "theories of practice"—we have to accept that teachers need to know some basics about theory prior to effectively determining sensible practices. This means learning new things, trying new strategies, and not doing what we've done that we can see is not working. The most obvious missing piece to this ECE workplace puzzle is early childhood–specific education.

Therefore, to talk about weaving theories of practice together in a meaningful way, we must first address the existing model of the ECE workplace and how it can be adapted. This is not an easy task to contemplate. There are many challenges to discussing the necessary changes we must make if we are to offer *all* of our children the start in life that they deserve.

I frequently change my mind about the order of addressing these changes. Lately, I've been thinking that these are the top two:

1. We need to reach consensus as a field on what the necessary improvements are and as a *group*, to get busy on implementing those improvements.

2. Any ordering of the necessary steps isn't going to take us where we need to be if we haven't identified a source of funding. And, as we are aware, we haven't identified a source of funding.

However, on the bright side, I have listened to focus groups discussing, disagreeing, and deliberating on all of the above, and that's *exciting*!

Chapter 4: Suggestions for Change, Questions to Ponder

"IMAGINE THE CHILD CARE of our dreams, not just child care that's good enough. Imagine if people working with young children received adequate professional preparation, opportunities for ongoing professional growth, and earnings equal to their investment in their careers" (Whitebook 2010, xix). I hope this quote from Marcy Whitebook inspires you as much as it inspires me.

As I return with energy to the issues of worthy wages, working conditions, and expected professional preparation for those who care for and teach young children, I can see that the many barriers we face are overwhelming. Marcy Whitebook has spent her career advocating for better understanding, working conditions, and wages for the early childhood workforce. In her paper "Finding a Better Way," Whitebook makes this point: "Even when advocates agree that the solution to the staffing crisis lies with a major public investment, the complexity of the current early childhood services delivery system creates many challenges. Because services are so decentralized, with multiple funding sources and regulatory requirements and because providers are so diverse with regard to professional preparation, location of care, and demographic characteristics, it is an especially daunting task to craft and fund policy reforms targeted to improving child care jobs" (Whitebook and Eichberg 2002, 4).

It is difficult, at best, to contemplate the kind of changes that would transpire if we were to restructure our approach to

73

providing services. And, take note that insisting on adequate training *will* restructure our approach. Yet if we go back to NAEYC's *Guiding Principles for the Development and Analysis of Early Childhood Public Policy* (1992, 1), several key points are already emphasized there for our field: "It is a public responsibility to set high-quality standards to safeguard *all* children in any form of out-of-home setting. Standards should address *staff qualifications, ongoing training requirements*, parent role, group size and staff-child ratios, discipline, health and safety aspects, and developmentally appropriate curriculum, and should be comparable for all out-of-home settings within the state" (emphases mine).

It has been a quarter of a century since these words were first drafted. Other points made in the same document include (all emphases mine):

- reducing turnover

- salary and benefits sufficient to attract and retain *qualified* staff

- salary and benefits should be comparable to those of other *professionals* with equivalent training and responsibilities

- must promote a stable, *qualified* early childhood workforce that meets *adequate* pre-service and *continuing education requirements*

Each of these reminds me of the Worthy Wage slogan: "Parents can't afford to pay. Teachers and providers can't afford to stay. There's got to be a better way."

Today the significant issues our field is facing remain the same. It saddens me to acknowledge that in some ways and places we are no further ahead on workforce development than we were twenty-five years ago. We have done significant work articulating how change should or could look, but we have not taken the steps to move beyond the status quo. We haven't insisted that teachers get the appropriate academic preparation to qualify them for wages equivalent to those of our public school teachers. It is even harder to accept mediocrity when the same quarter of a century has provided us with an explosion of new knowledge about what *all* children need and deserve.

This is not a "Which comes first?" scenario. We cannot expect or advocate for public school educators' salaries for a workforce with high school diplomas or "some" college. We know what has to come first. Because the private sector operates so many programs for children and the need is so great, an immediate transition is impossible. If we want professional salaries, we need to do the professional training that merits that compensation. But beginning the conversation civilly, respectfully, *and* publicly would be a start. The outline for discussion is pretty clear for those who have continually followed the problem for decades:

- Quality programs are based on the strong body of knowledge about how children grow and learn.

- That knowledge (ECE theory), when understood and implemented, gives children a good start in life and reduces challenging behavior.

- The majority of the ECE workforce is not adequately grounded in this theory.

- If teachers don't know the theory, they can't practice it.

- To improve the lives of all children, this needs to change.

75

The other significant pieces of the conversation (debate? dilemma?) are the barriers to moving forward. I've discussed them in previous chapters, but they are worth repeating here:

- Quality care and education are expensive. We have no sustainable identified funding source to create the system our children deserve.

- A large and vocal population still believes that enjoying children, finding them cute, and having a nice day with them are all that is necessary for those who form the early childhood workforce.

- Many practitioners and parents don't understand the importance of theories of ECE practice to quality care, so they have no motivation to find out more about it.

- As long as the differential between well-trained and untrained teachers is almost nonexistent, no monetary motivation exists for the change we need.

One Possible Solution

When I was an early childhood center director, I told staff I was always willing to hear their complaints as long as they also offered some possible solutions. So the very writing of this book creates ambivalence for me. It is hard to complain about what's now known:

- Professional early childhood workers know that teacher training and quality education for all children are related.

- Decades of research documents that too few of our workforce have this quality training.

- Many workers do not believe they need more education, and even if they want to pursue a degree, their wages do not allow them to pay college tuition.

- At this time, there is no identifiable funding in place to remedy this serious challenge to the health and well-being of children in the United States.

As for a solution to these complaints: I propose that it would be a step forward for the profession to adopt a unified position on the qualifications expected of individuals intending to be early childhood teachers. This should actually be implemented. Yet just as Stephanie Feeney (2012) has pointed out, in our attempts to be inclusive and to welcome diversity, we hedge on a single description of quality.

> I propose that it would be a step forward for the profession to adopt a unified position on the qualifications expected of individuals intending to be early childhood teachers.

Teachers, administrators, and ECE professors also hedge on what expectations we have of those who teach. We say, "Ideally, our teachers should be well educated in early childhood theories of practice," and then we accept the status quo, implying that higher goals can't be reached. What if we were to place children who receive state funding for child care only in programs in which a stated percentage—at least 50 percent—of the teachers have a bachelor's degree? This would echo the bold requirements made by Head Start in recent years. It is only one step, but it would be forward movement.

As human beings, we all deserve respect, courtesy, and acknowledgment for our contributions. It is not a good idea, however, to rely on the input of an assistant teacher with an associate's degree in ECE to carry the same weight as a seasoned professional who has worked in ECE for thirty years, raised a family, and holds an earned doctorate in child growth and development when making a decision about a child's future. If we compare ourselves to the medical profession, we know that an LNA (licensed nursing assistant) does not administer anesthesia to a patient prior to brain surgery; it is accepted that there are different levels of expertise. It is accepted that many bright medical students might be right on the same page as a surgeon on some issues, but they are not allowed to operate. It is also accepted that it would be absurd for a LNA to expect the same compensation as a brain surgeon.

There have been significant efforts made on the part of many ECE professionals to establish and encourage professional lattices and compensation schedules. I applaud these and have been part of some of them. Examples, however, of actual, systemic progress made in academic preparation and anticipated salary ranges to make that effort worthwhile are in short supply. We all know the most frequently cited reason for this lack of progress: Who is going to pay?

I'd like to return to Marcy Whitebook (2010, xix). The child care of our dreams is a place where people working with young children receive

- adequate professional preparation,

- opportunities for ongoing professional growth, and

- earnings equal to their investment in their careers.

It seems to me that those of us who choose to work in the ECE field need to accept and acquire the adequate professional preparation Whitebook refers to. We also need to seek out access to ongoing professional growth opportunities. Finally, ECE workers need to agree to accept, as other professions do, that earnings should be related to education and experience.

After sharing my own story at a regional conference, several colleagues suggested I include it in the book because it really is related. Colleagues have suggested to me that my own career goals and directions are a good example of the education/experience dilemma.

I have a bachelor of arts in elementary education and a master of education in early childhood education. I completed all of the coursework for a doctorate in sociology of the family. For a variety of reasons, I chose to discontinue my final work on that degree. I had taught in both the state college system and at the university for many years when I entered the doctoral program. Many years ago, it was possible to get much teaching work at that level with only a master's degree. I had won a distinguished faculty award. But times and policies change, and that option is not as open today.

By the time I started my doctoral studies in sociology, I was very accustomed to having my own group of college students to guide. But every day I would take attendance, take notes, and grade papers and exams for the professor to whom I had been assigned as a teaching assistant (TA). That is what was required by the department. It never occurred to me to say I was quite capable of teaching a college class myself and had been doing so for twenty years. I knew the rules. If I wanted a doctorate, I could pay for one or be a teaching assistant. That was policy. I would sometimes walk across campus to the child and family studies building to teach if someone was out on maternity leave. In one building, I was a college instructor; three buildings down, I was a TA. I knew the rules of the game and abided by them.

I am the mother of four children. I went back to the university for a semester after my last child was born, but I decided that I did not want to balance my life so precariously, so I withdrew from the program. I wanted to be at home when my teenagers had friends over. I wanted dinner to be peaceful, not rushed. It was my choice to have four children, but it was more work than I'd anticipated it would be. I wanted the time to enjoy

79

them, go hiking, play with my youngest. It became impossible to do all of the above while doing the gradings, study, and TA responsibility. I always assumed I would go back sometime, but I never did. I have continued, off and on, to work as adjunct faculty. I am a good teacher, and it is certainly easier for me to teach college than to teach four-year-olds. Instead, I chose to work where I could be with my youngest daughter, watching her grow.

Sometimes former students or teachers who still consider me to be their mentor say they think I should teach college because I have such a passion for the field and a direct way of presenting what needs to be mastered. When they do say these things, I am quick to reply, "When I was teaching you, I could get away with being an instructor with a master's. Today you need an earned doctorate." Often they say, "That's just not fair, you are so good at it!" My reply is always the same: "It is too fair. It is too difficult for a university to decide on an individual basis, 'She has experience, maybe we could hire her.' They need specific requirements for the job. If I wanted to be a professor for the rest of my life, I should have stuck with the doctoral program." I did not.

I don't consider myself lacking because I didn't finish the doctorate. I made a choice I would make again. Do I have the intelligence to finish such a program? Yes. Would it make a huge difference in my life today? No. Now and again, I think of Kurt Vonnegut, who stacked up his books, took them to the University of Chicago, and said he thought they were as good as a dissertation! I've no idea if it would work, but I made choices and live with them. End of story. I find work I can do with a master of education.

It is possible (though perhaps not legal) for a relative who is not a licensed electrician but competent at such things to put outlets in your house. Sometimes the work might be done better than a licensed electrician would do . . . but I'd rather go with the licensed electrician. Requiring certain standards before being allowed to do certain kinds of work makes sense. There needs to be a basement below which we are not willing to go. It doesn't mean one person is a better person than another. It means one person is more qualified as an electrician than another. And for those of you saying, "I had lots of PhD professors who stunk"—that is what

People can be fired because of their lack of competence. People should not be hired because of their lack of credentials.

performance evaluations are for. People can be fired because of their lack of competence. People should not be hired because of their lack of credentials. That means me at the university . . . and some of you working with children.

Certainly requiring a degree of all teachers does not eliminate the possibility that plenty of teachers with degrees will be incompetent anyway. That has always been the case. But as I've said, it is not nearly as frequent as proponents of conventional wisdom would have us believe. From the 1979 Day Care Study to Whitebook's current work, the data clearly falls on the side of increased quality when everyone teaching young children has earned a degree in ECE. We have settled for too little for too long. Children deserve more from us.

Where Can We Go from Here?

It is not easy to determine policy for important segments of our society or culture. As early educators, we are in the position of needing to accept this responsibility, whether we want to or not.

As an educator with forty years of experience in the field, I am in the position of seeing patterns—negative and positive—that the field has engaged in over the past several decades. There are several statements I can make, in conclusion, with some confidence:

- Children rely on adults to act in their best interest.

- Research in the past quarter century documents what is in the best interest of children.

- What is in the best interest of children is not always convenient for the rest of us.

- We have a professional responsibility to respond to what we know is in the best interest of children.

In conclusion, I'd like to acknowledge that much of what I've written here is bound to upset someone. I know this to be true, if for no other reason, than the cautious tone of voice in which practitioners and colleagues from many disciplines have responded to my inquiries about professionalism, credentials, and day-to-day work with young children. There is no easy answer to the dilemmas our field is facing.

As I've spoken with lawyers, congressional delegates, teachers, parents, students, and advocates over the past year, I've learned how many dilemmas we must face before finding resolutions to the questions before us.

Here are some of these questions:

- How much education do adults need to provide optimal learning environments for the young?

- If we know what needs to be done but don't know how to fund it, what are we supposed to do?

82

- If we suddenly require degrees of all those who educate other people's children, aren't we insulting the people who have done it for years without this education?

- Who will pay for the changes programs will need to undergo to align them with what we know is best for children?

- What kind of time frame should be allowed for us to transition from a workforce of untrained labor to a skilled labor force?

- What kind of choices will be available to those presently working without the necessary credentials?

- Will this new infrastructure provide jobs and a meaningful place for adults who enjoy children and have no desire to continue their own formal education?

- How do we organize ourselves to begin this very important conversation within our professional field?

- What is needed to focus national attention on these issues and win acceptance of its critical importance to families with young children and to the future of our country?

Many questions need to be answered. Some of them have already been answered but not responded to. The time to advocate for the youngest children is now! My call for action is for everyone who works with children: those of us who never finished our doctorate or master's degree, those of us who went to work to be with our own preschoolers and never left, those of us who don't really enjoy children that much and should move on, those of us who need more education but can't afford it (find it!), and those of us who teach third grade because we need the money but know our best work happened in kindergarten!

Conclusions:

- The challenges are many!

- The solutions will probably be slow in coming.

- The information I have included here will, no doubt, be misunderstood by many.

- I suggest Stephanie Feeney's book *Professionalism in Early Childhood Education* to both new and very experienced teachers who want to review the NAEYC's Code of Ethical Conduct.

- As professionals, we have *core values* about being committed to doing our best for children. We talk with each other about keeping children safe, nurturing their love of nature, helping them learn to get along, coaching them in their coping skills through and after disappointments. We consider these to be professional responsibilities.

If we don't know something, we can't be held responsible for making poor choices, for taking ineffective roads to solving problems. If we've been given information, our responsibility changes. If we know the effective route to a positive outcome, then our responsibility to achieve it is greater.

If we can't achieve it, we probably still have the professional responsibility to discuss it, respectfully disagree, and explore solutions. Anything less could be viewed as avoiding our professional responsibilities. . . . Let's talk.

References

Bassok, Daphna, Maria Fitzpatrick, Susanna Loeb, and Agustina S. Paglayan. 2013. "The Early Childhood Care and Education Workforce from 1990 through 2010: Changing Dynamics and Persistent Concerns." *Education Finance and Policy* 8 (4): 581–601.

Delpit, Lisa. 2006. *Other People's Children: Cultural Conflict in the Classroom.* New York: New Press.

Didion, Joan. 2012. *Blue Nights.* New York: Vintage Books.

Feeney, Stephanie. 2012. *Professionalism in Early Childhood Education: Doing Our Best for Young Children.* Boston: Pearson Education.

Goffin, Stacie G. 2013. *Early Childhood Education for a New Era: Leading for our Profession.* New York: Teachers College Press.

Katz, Lilian. 1977. *Talks with Teachers: Reflections on Early Childhood Education.* Washington, DC: National Association for the Education of Young Children.

Kohl, Herbert E. 1984. *Growing Minds: On Becoming a Teacher.* New York: Harper and Row.

Morgan, Gwen. 1986. *The National State of Child Care Regulation.* Work Family Directions Incorporated.

NAEYC (National Association for the Education of Young Children). 1992. *Guiding Principles for the Development and Analysis of Early Childhood Public Policy: A Position Statement of the National Association for the Education of Young Children.* Washington, DC: NAEYC.

———. 2009. *Where We Stand: On Professional Preparation Standards.* Washington, DC: NAEYC. www.naeyc.org/files/naeyc/files/2009Where WeStandStandardsrev4_12.pdf.

Papalia, Diane E., Sally Wendkos Olds, and Ruth Duskin Feldman. 1987. *A Child's World: Infancy through Adolescence,* 4th ed. New York: McGraw-Hill.

References

Ruopp, Richard, J. Travers, F. Glantz, and C. Coelen. 1979. *Children at the Center: Final Report of the National Day Care Study*. Cambridge, MA: Abt Associates.

Smith, Kristin, and Reagan Baughman. 2007. "Low Wages Prevalent in Direct Care and Child Care Workforce." The Carsey Institute at the Scholars' Repository. Paper 25.

Whitebook, Marcy. 2010. Foreword to the first edition of *The Visionary Director*, 2nd ed., xix–xxii. St. Paul, MN: Redleaf Press.

Whitebook, Marcy, and Abby Eichberg. 2002. "Finding a Better Way: Defining and Assessing Public Policies to Improve Child Care Workforce Compensation." Center for the Study of Child Care Employment. http://www.irle.berkeley.edu/cscce/wp-content/uploads/2001/01/betterway.pdf.

Whitebook, Marcy. 1990. "Who Cares? Child Care Teachers and the Quality of Care in America." http://www.irle.berkeley.edu/cscce/wp-content/uploads/2010/07/Who-Cares-full-report.pdf.

Index

87

About the Author

CAROL GARHART MOONEY BEGAN her teaching career in the inner city of Richmond, Virginia. As a college student, she volunteered in programs to involve children and families in their own communities. She also volunteered in 1965 at the first trial run of Head Start programs in Washington, DC.

Carol worked for nearly fifteen years for Head Start programs in New Hampshire, first as an itinerant instructor for the New Hampshire Head Start CDA program, and later as a manager and transition specialist for Belknap-Merrimack Head Start. She has supervised student and practicing educators for more than twenty-five years. She also served as one of the first child care administrators for the New Hampshire Department of Health and Human Services.

Carol taught college for many years and was empathetic toward her students, many of whom, like herself, were raising families, working, and going to college at the same time. She set about a project of condensing volumes of educational research into an easier-to-read format, combining real classroom examples with theoretical positions. The first of these, *Theories of Childhood*, was published many years ago, and is one of Redleaf Press's best-selling textbooks. It has sold more than sixty thousand copies in the United States and thirteen other countries. The second, *Theories of Attachment*, was published several years ago.

The last of the trilogy, *Theories of Teaching Young Children*, will be published in 2015. Carol has also written *Use Your Words*, a more humorous and practical book for teachers, and *Swinging Pendulums: Cautionary Tales for Early Educators*.

Carol has been awarded the Distinguished Faculty Award for teaching at Granite State College and continues her work with children and families as a state adviser to Project LAUNCH (Linking Actions for Unmet Needs in Children's Health). She is a past president of New Hampshire Association for the Education of Young Children and past board member of Early Learning New Hampshire.

She is the mother of four grown children and grandmother of three growing children. In her spare time, she enjoys kayaking with her husband, Marc, and entertaining her large group of grown children and their children!